TOP **10**
NAPLES AND THE AMALFI COAST

CONTENTS

NAPLES AND THE AMALFI COAST

INTRODUCING

Colourful houses on the island of Procida

WELCOME TO
NAPLES AND THE AMALFI COAST

Combining captivating urban energy, natural beauty and chic style, Naples and the Amalfi Coast is a destination unlike anywhere else. Don't want to miss a thing? With Top 10 Naples and the Amalfi Coast, you'll enjoy the very best the region has to offer.

"See Naples and die," wrote German poet Johann Wolfgang von Goethe as he undertook his Grand Tour. Goethe was just one of many visitors who was bewitched by the unrivalled energy of Naples. One of the world's oldest cities, here Baroque churches rest above ancient catacombs, and winding alleys lead past ornate palazzos, relics of an era when the

A scooter navigates the busy streets of central Naples

city was a major economic and military power. Its age of royal dominance may have passed, but Naples remains a cosmopolitan cultural hub: its cobbled streets and piazzas are endearingly chaotic, as locals dart past on scooters or eat margheritas in the storied birthplace of pizza. Esteemed galleries housing the masterworks of Caravaggio sit snug alongside riotous bars serving spritz to a huge, global crowd – it's all part of the exuberant urban alchemy that is Naples.

Above it all, the brooding hulk of Mount Vesuvius looms, with the preserved ancient towns of Pompeii and Herculaneum testament to the volcano's formidable power. Further along the Amalfi Coast, lapped by the azure waters of the Tyrrhenian Sea, lie kaleidoscopic towns like Positano and Ravello, with their hip boutiques and charming gardens. Just a short ferry ride away, the thermal spas of Ischia, the coastal caves of Capri and the beautiful pastel houses of Procida lie waiting.

So, where to start? With Top 10 Naples and the Amalfi Coast, of course. This pocket-sized guide gets to the heart of the region with simple lists of 10, expert local knowledge and comprehensive maps, helping you turn an ordinary trip into an extraordinary one.

THE STORY OF
NAPLES AND THE AMALFI COAST

One of the oldest inhabited cities in the world, Naples has been a centre of culture for millennia. It has witnessed the rise and fall of countless rulers, attracted by the city's riches and the natural beauty of the surrounding coast. Here's the story of how it came to be.

Early engraving of the Greek town of Neapolis

Greeks and Romans
The region around Naples was settled by Greeks in the second millennium BCE, with a town that was initially named after the goddess Parthenope. Neapolis (New City)– the embryo of modern Naples – was founded in 470 BCE. Around 326 BCE, the city and surrounding area were conquered by territory-hungry Romans. The idyllic setting of Neapolis and the surrounding coastline made the region a *buen retiro* for wealthy intellectuals, and sublime resort towns like Pompeii were constructed to facilitate the Roman good life. Everything changed in 79 CE when Mount Vesuvius erupted. Within a few hours, the region was covered by ash and boiling volcanic mud, with many inhabitants killed in wealthy towns like Pompeii and Herculaneum. When the Roman Empire fell in the 5th century, Byzantine general Flavius Belisarius conquered the western Roman Empire.

The eruption of Vesuvius in 79 CE led to huge destruction

Pope Clement IV crowns King Charles I of Anjou

Norman Conquest

By the early 12th century, the Normans had gained control of much of Italy and Sicily, establishing the new Kingdom of Sicily. The Norman king, Roger II, conquered Naples, and his rule ushered in a period of major prosperity for the city, though his court was based in Palermo. Naples was not to be controlled by Sicily for long. In the mid-13th century, Pope Clement IV assigned both Naples and the wider Kingdom of Sicily to the French Anjou dynasty, who shifted power back to Naples and constructed many lavish new buildings like the Castel Nuovo.

New World Wealth

Due to losing territory to the Anjous, Sicilian resentment came to a head in 1282. A riot against Anjou rule, known as the Sicilian Vespers, spread from the island, initiating a 20-year war which ended with two kingdoms: that of Sicily and that of Naples, which would last until 1816. During that time Europe's royal families fought over territory, and control of the Kingdom of Naples fell to the French, then the Spanish, then the Austrian Habsburgs and finally the Spanish Bourbons. The Kingdom became an important source of economic and military power for the Spanish Crown and by the beginning of the 17th century, Naples was Europe's largest city and cultural hotspot, with a population of 300,000.

Moments in History

2 CE
Emperor Augustus opens the Neapolitan Isolympic Games, an equivalent to those held at Olympia in Greece.

536
The Byzantine army under Belisarius lays siege to Naples and captures the city.

1224
Holy Roman emperor Frederick II founds the University of Naples to offset the dominant influence of the university at Bologna.

1279
Charles I of Anjou moves the royal residence of Naples from Castel Capuano to Castel Nuovo.

1656
Six months after plague strikes, three-quarters of Naples' inhabitants are dead and buried in mass graves.

1816
Naples becomes the capital of the new Kingdom of the Two Sicilies.

1860
Naples votes to join a newly unified Italy under Italian king Vittorio Emanuele II.

1980
A huge earthquake at Irpinia kills least 2,483 people in the region.

2017
Naples mayor Luigi de Magistris receives the Valerioti-Impastato award for his work against crime and corruption.

2023
Naples and the Amalfi Coast record their best year for tourism. The city received 12.4 million people through its airport and 1.6 million cruise passengers.

2024
Naples inaugurates Line 6 of its metro network, 11 years after the line closed due to a building collapse. The re-opened line sees Chiaia station added to the city's Art Stations circuit.

The cholera epidemic in 1884 claims thousands of lives

An Enlightened City

In 1734 the Spanish king Charles III of Bourbon arrived in Naples. He invested huge energy and expense in the city, turning Naples into a thriving engine of the Enlightenment. He built the Villa di Capodimonte (*p32*) and the Teatro di San Carlo (*p94*), among other grand buildings. The renovated city thrived, attracting leading composers and philosophers. French troops interrupted this cultural flourishing, however, by seizing control in 1799, forming the Parthenopean Republic, and by 1806, Napoleon Bonaparte had conquered the entire Kingdom of Naples. The Bourbon monarch, Ferdinand IV, was instated as King of Naples and Sicily and in 1816 Naples became the capital of the new Kingdom of the Two Sicilies.

Unification with Italy

This era of shifting kingdoms was to be forever ended by Giuseppe Garibaldi, commander of the Italian unification movement. He entered Naples in 1860 to gather support for unification, and in October, Naples voted to join a united Italy under the rule of Italian king, Vittorio Emanuele II. After unification, Naples lost much of the importance it had held for centuries, as power was confined to the wealthier north. Cholera epidemics in 1884 and 1910–11 and a wave of industrialization inspired modernizing reforms in the 19th century, but these efforts were insufficient to combat the damaging effects of World War I (1915–18). The rise of Benito Mussolini and his fascist regime, along with the Depression of the 1930s, saw Naples further reduced in influence compared to the north.

Mount Vesuvius spewing ash shortly after Allied arrival, 1944

World War II

The Nazis occupied Naples in 1943 after the fall of Mussolini, but it became the first city to rise up against military occupation. The famously passionate Neapolitans were incensed by German threats to deport all young men, so they rose against their occupiers in what became known as the Four Days of Naples. Some even claim that the Allied offensive of 1944 was only successful because the Germans were kept so busy subduing the city's rioters. Naples took a long time to recover from the heavy Allied bombing raids of 1940 to 1943, and the region suffered from mass post-war unemployment. Like much of southern Italy, Naples fell prey to organized crime in the shape of the Mafia, who were quick to capitalize on this poverty. The local Camorra organisation gained power after the Irpinia earthquake in 1980, when much of the aid fell into their hands.

The Region Today

Naples' reputation has improved massively thanks to increased local spending and improved transport links. This regeneration has seen it become the setting for TV shows such as *Ripley* (2024) and *My Brilliant Friend* (2018–24). The wider Amalfi Coast, meanwhile, remains one of the most popular holiday destinations in Italy, with tourists flocking to affluent coastal resorts just as their ancient ancestors did 2,000 years ago.

Charming houses on the island of Procida in the Bay of Naples

TOP 10
EXPERIENCES

Planning the perfect trip to Naples and the Amalfi Coast? Whether you're visiting for the first time or making a return trip, there are some things you simply shouldn't miss. To make the most of your time – and to enjoy the very best this diverse stretch of coast has to offer – be sure to try these experiences.

1 People watch in a piazza

The many piazzas of Naples – Piazza del Plebiscito, Piazza Trieste and Piazza Dante, to name a few – offer the perfect place to unwind, perhaps with a very Neapolitan shot of espresso or Aperol spritz. Any and every piazza is the perfect place to see all of local life play out in front of you.

2 Marvel at Caravaggio

The art world's original rebel, Caravaggio fled to Naples from Malta in the last years of his life. The city is home to three of his works – *The Seven Works of Mercy*, *The Flagellation of Christ* and *The Martyrdom of Saint Ursula* – as well as countless tales of the artist's riotous misdeeds.

3 Visit the opera

Home to the oldest continuously active opera house in the world, the Teatro di San Carlo *(p94)*, Naples has long been synonymous with opera. Catch a performance at the Teatro, where you can take in the architecture and spectacular music surrounded by elegantly dressed Neapolitans.

4 Go shopping

Naples is a shopper's paradise, with many of Italy's chicest designs on display. The options for retail therapy are endless: browse boutiques on Via Toledo, size up divine dresses on Via San Gregorio Armeno, stop by artisan stores on Via dei Tribunali or visit upmarket shops in Galleria Umberto I.

5 Head underground

The long history of Naples is layered like strata beneath the streets. Riddled with catacombs, tunnels and caves dating to Greco-Roman times, the subterranean network comprises Napoli Sotterranea (p66), the Galleria Borbonica and La Neapolis Sotterrata.

6 Explore cathedrals

The region is home to churches that run the gamut from the beautiful to the bizarre. The majolica-tiled dome of Chiesa di Santa Maria Assunta soars over Positano (p45), while the Duomo (p26) in Naples is said to house the blood of a saint.

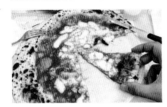

7 Eat pizza

Naples is inarguably the home of pizza and, whisper it, you can eat the best pizza margherita in the world here. Each is made by the best chefs from San Marzano tomatoes grown on volcanic soil and buffalo mozzarella from the Campania region.

8 Watch a sunset

Top off a busy day by looking over the blue waters of the Bay of Naples from the ramparts of the ancient fortress of Castel dell'Ovo (p94). Bring a picnic or grab an aperitivo at one of the bars along the *lungomare* – the seafront strip – on Via Partenope.

9 Lounge on the beach

Home to some of Italy's finest beaches, the Amalfi Coast and islands are the perfect place to relax on golden sands. Whether you kick back at Spiaggia Grande near Positano or take to the sands of Ischia, you'll be charmed by the region's coastline.

10 Time travel at Pompeii

The affluent Roman city and holiday resort of Pompeii (p38) was destroyed when Vesuvius erupted in 79 CE. What remains is a vast city frozen in time, offering an eerie snapshot of life in ancient Rome, with an array of bars, brothels and private residences.

ITINERARIES

Visiting Pompeii, seeing the Blue Grotto or tucking into a pizza: there's a lot to see and do in Naples and the Amalfi Coast. With places to eat, drink or take in the view, these itineraries offer ways to spend 2 days and 4 days in the region.

2 DAYS IN NAPLES

Day 1

Morning

To appreciate royal Naples, begin your day at the city's largest square, the Piazza del Plebiscito (p93). On one side is the church of San Francesco di Paola, built to resemble the Pantheon in Rome; on the other is the lavish Palazzo Reale (p22), once the centre of power in southern Italy. It's time to fuel yourself with an espresso; head to the grand 19th-century coffee house, Gran Caffè Gambrinus (p99). From here, it's a short walk over to Castel Nuovo (p24), the city's imposing medieval fortress; inside you can enjoy the Museo Civico. Now for that definitive Neapolitan experience: pizza. Stop by Brandi (p99), birthplace of the classic margherita.

> **DRINK**
> Looh out for Italian DOCG wines, which are of top quality. In the Campania region, there are several produced in Benevento and Avellino, and you'll find them served in the pizzerias and smaller wine bars around Tribunali.

Afternoon

With a full belly, it's time to head along Spaccanapoli (p82), the lively main street that traverses the city's historic centre. As you take in the chaos of this thoroughfare, watch out for mopeds weaving in and out of the crowd. Find some respite from the bustle with a visit to Sansevero Chapel (p84) to see the Veiled Christ, a life-size marble statue covered in a seemingly transparent shroud. Note that you'll need to book tickets in advance to see the statue. There's more art to see at the Duomo (p26), the city's gargantuan Gothic cathedral. Finish with a spritz and bowl of pasta at a restaurant in lively Tribunali.

Day 2

Morning

Start the day by wandering the Centro Storico, stopping for a caffè and crispy cornetto pastry in Piazza Bellini (p84). Refreshed, head along to the Museo Archeologico Nazionale (p28), which houses a trove of statues, mosaics and

San Francesco di Paola
in Piazza del Plebiscito

artifacts from Pompeii and other ancient sites. When you're ready to leave the world of the ancients, enjoy a street-food lunch – *pizza fritta* (fried pizza) or *cuoppo di pesce fritto* (a cone filled with fried fish) – from a spot on Via dei Tribunali.

Afternoon
After lunch, you'll head underground. Walk towards the San Gennaro tunnels to visit the catacombs *(p66)*, with burials dating back to the 2nd century. Now, head for the heights: take the funicular up to Castel Sant'Elmo *(p95)* on Vomero hill to watch the sun set. Later, enjoy dinner by the romantic Borgo Marinari, admiring the Castel dell'Ovo *(p94)*, which keeps its watchful eye over the entire Bay of Naples.

Enjoying a slice of fried pizza on the street in Naples

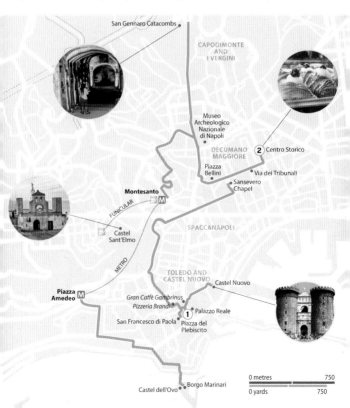

San Gennaro Catacombs

CAPODIMONTE AND I VERGINI

Museo Archeologico Nazionale di Napoli

DECUMANO MAGGIORE

Piazza Bellini

2 Centro Storico

Via dei Tribunali

Sansevero Chapel

Montesanto Ⓜ

FUNICULAR

Castel Sant'Elmo

SPACCANAPOLI

METRO

TOLEDO AND CASTEL NUOVO

Castel Nuovo

Piazza Amedeo Ⓜ

Gran Caffè Gambrinus
Pizzeria Brandi

1 Palazzo Reale

San Francesco di Paola

Piazza del Plebiscito

| 0 metres | 750 |
| 0 yards | 750 |

Castel dell'Ovo • Borgo Marinari

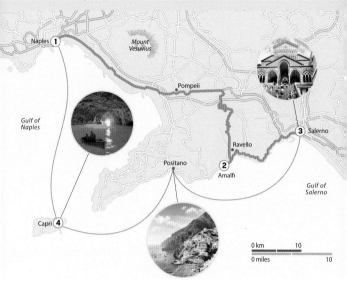

4 DAYS ON THE AMALFI COAST

Ancient thoroughfare in the heart of Pompeii

Day 1

Take the train or drive from Naples to Pompeii (p38); the train takes a little over half an hour. Today will be spent slowly exploring the many wonders of the ancient city. It's best to arrive early in the morning to avoid the crowds and the punishing heat in summer. Take time to admire the Forum, the vast amphitheatre, the colourful frescoes decorating the House of the Faun and the artwork in the various villas – the

> **EAT**
>
> Amalfi is known for its wonderfully juicy lemons, used in limoncello. You can also try out *delizie al limone*, creamy lemon-flavoured cakes.

longer you linger, the more your imagination will run wild. The restaurants are outside the park grounds so you can have lunch in the cafeteria or eat a packed lunch in one of the picnic areas. Take the train back to Naples for dinner and a *passeggiata* along the Lungomare, the pedestrianized seafront walkway.

Day 2

Transfer your base to the Amalfi Coast. It's about 90 minutes' drive to the pretty seaside town of Amalfi (p44) along the Costiera Amalfitana (Amalfi Drive), a picturesque stretch of a road winding alongside the dramatic cliffs above the sea. Once you arrive in Amalfi, visit the fascinating Museo

SHOP
Capri is famous for hand-made sandals. Visit a sandal shop like Canfora (Via Camerelle, 3), where a cobbler measures your feet while you choose your straps.

della Carta (*p55*) and the iconic Cathedral of St Andrew that overlooks Piazza Duomo (*p53*), a perfect place to enjoy pasta from one of the small restaurants. In the afternoon, grab a *gelato* and take a walk along Marina Grande – if the sun is shining, you can even have a swim. Afterwards, drive up the mountain road beyond Amalfi to visit the peaceful town of Ravello (*p45*), where you can enjoy beautiful views from Villa Cimbrone and a fine dinner at the Villa Maria restaurant (*p61*). Either head back to Amalfi for the evening or stay in Ravello.

Day 3

This morning, it's time to head further along the coast, and with views like these, you'll want to drive slowly. Head along to Salerno (*p106*), where you can take a stroll on the Lungomare Trieste to take in the wonders of the town. After a light lunch, take a slow ferry to Positano, the "Vertical City", for a night at Le Sirenuse (*p132*), one of the most romantic hotels on the coast, with views of the pastel-coloured houses that cling to the cliffside.

Day 4

The chic island of Capri (*p42*) is today's destination. Have breakfast in Positano, then catch a high-speed ferry to the island, which takes around 90 minutes. When you arrive at Marina Grande, have a coffee, then take a boat tour that visits the Blue Grotto, an echoing sea cave lapped by azure waters. Get off the boat at Anacapri and take the chairlift to Monte Solaro, the highest point on Capri; from here, you can admire Mount Vesuvius, the Faraglioni Rocks, Ischia, Sorrento and the Bay of Naples, before a relaxing lunch at Casa Orlandi (*Via Giuseppe Orlandi, 38/40*). Take a bus into Capri Town for your last evening, starting with some shopping on Via Camerelle. To finish, people watch over an aperitivo in the Piazzetta, before taking a ferry back to Naples.

The sublime Blue Grotto cave, Capri

TOP 10 HIGHLIGHTS

Statue near the forum of Pompeii

EXPLORE THE
HIGHLIGHTS

There are some sights in Naples and on the Amalfi Coast that you simply shouldn't miss, and it's these attractions that make the Top 10. Discover what makes each one a must-see on the following pages.

❶ Palazzo Reale

❷ Castel Nuovo

❸ Duomo

❹ Museo Archeologico Nazionale

❺ Museo di Capodimonte

❻ Certosa e Museo di San Martino

❼ Pompeii

❽ Capri

❾ Amalfi, Ravello and Positano

❿ Paestum

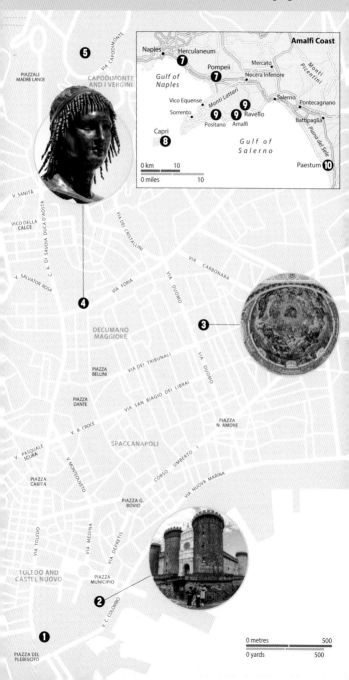

5

PIAZZALE
MADRE LANDI

VIA CAPODIMONTE

CAPODIMONTE
AND I VERGINI

Naples

Herculaneum **7**

Pompeii **7**

Mercato

Nocera Inferiore

Gulf of
Naples

Vico Equense

Monti Lattari

Monti Picentini

Salerno

Pontecagnano

Sorrento

9

Ravello **9**

Battipaglia

Positano **9**

Amalfi

Capri **8**

Gulf of
Salerno

Piana del Sele

Paestum **10**

| 0 km | 10 |
| 0 miles | 10 |

V. SANITÀ

VICO DELLA
CALCE

C.A DI SAVOIA DUCA D'AOSTA

VIA DEI CRISTALLINI

V. SALVATOR ROSA

VIA FORIA

VIA DUOMO

VIA CARBONARA

4

3

DECUMANO
MAGGIORE

PIAZZA
BELLINI

VIA DEI TRIBUNALI

VIA DUOMO

PIAZZA
DANTE

VIA SAN BIAGIO DEI LIBRAI

V. B. CROCE

PIAZZA
N. AMORE

V. PASQUALE
SCURA

V. MONTEOLIVETO

SPACCANAPOLI

CORSO UMBERTO I

PIAZZA
CARITÀ

VIA NUOVA MARINA

PIAZZA G.
BOVIO

V. TOLEDO

VIA MEDINA

VIA DEPRETIS

TOLEDO AND
CASTEL NUOVO

PIAZZA
MUNICIPIO

2

V. C. COLOMBO

1

PIAZZA DEL
PLEBISCITO

| 0 metres | 500 |
| 0 yards | 500 |

The "Scalone d'Onore", Palazzo Reale's grand staircase

PALAZZO REALE

🗺 N5 🏛 Piazza del Plebiscito 1 📞 081 580 82 55 🕐 9am–7pm Thu–Tue

This imposing royal palace is testament to Naples' historic status as one of Europe's most important cities. Construction on the Baroque building began in 1600, and the Palazzo Reale has since seen numerous improvements and redesigns over the centuries. The grand throne room alone makes it clear that this was one of the most important courts in the Mediterranean in the 17th century. The palace remained a significant royal residence until 1946, when the Italian monarchy was exiled for its support of fascist leader Benito Mussolini.

1 Façade
Dominating the vast Piazza del Plebiscito, the palace's late Renaissance façade of brickwork and grey piperno stone is decorated with giant statues of Naples' foremost kings.

2 Teatro di Corte
Dating back to the 1768, this beautiful private theatre stands as a testament to the royal family's passion for comic opera. In the side niches are 12 figures crafted by artist Angelo Viva that depict Apollo and his Muses.

3 Staircase
A monumental staircase leads from the central courtyard up to the royal apartments. The original masterpiece dates from 1651; in 1837 it was embellished with pink and white marble.

4 Cappella Palatina
A 16th-century wooden door, painted in faux bronze, leads to the Royal Chapel, where the court's religious activities took place. The high altar consists of semiprecious stones set in gilt copper, while the 18th-century nativity scene is a study of local life at the time.

5 Sala di Ercole
The ornate Hall of Hercules derives its name from an ancient statue that was on display here in the 19th century.

DRINK
Gran Caffè Gambrinus (p99), located in a stylish piazza next to the palace, is an excellent choice for a drink, snacks or a full meal.

**Palazzo Reale
Site Plan**

6 Paintings

Of considerable importance are the palace's abundant paintings, including works by Giordano, Guercino, Carracci, Preti and Titian. Also worthy of interest are 17th-century Dutch portraits, 18th-century Chinese watercolours and 19th-century Neapolitan landscape paintings.

7 Furnishings

Fine examples of historic furniture

predominate in the palace's apartments, much of it of French manufacture. Tapestries adorn many rooms, as do exceptional examples of 18th-century marble tables, elaborately inlaid with semi-precious stones.

8 Decor of the Apartments

A series of vibrant frescoes adorn the 30 royal apartments, each chosen to enhance the luxury of the suites.

9 Biblioteca Nazionale

In the eastern wing, the massive National Library has at its core the Farnese Collection, with books dating from the 5th century. Also here are 1st-century-BCE papyri found at Herculaneum.

10 Hanging Garden

The palace's 19th-century style roof garden offers great views across the bay and features flowers and shrubs in keeping with the original planting scheme. It underwent a €35 million renovation before it reopened to the public in 2018.

PALACE GUIDE

You are free to walk around the inner courtyard and gardens of the Palazzo Reale at your leisure without a ticket. There is a charge to enter the palace, however, and visitors must follow a set itinerary once inside. Booking ahead is advised in the high season (coopculture.it).

Clockwise from right
A marble table in the royal apartments; impressive ceiling fresco; Teatro di Corte; façade of the Palazzo Reale

CASTEL NUOVO

📍 N5 🏛 Piazza Municipio 🕐 8:30am–6:30pm Mon–Sat 🌐 italia.it/en/campania/naples/castel-nuovo-maschio-angioino

The Castel Nuovo, known locally as the Maschio Angioino, was officially called the "New Castle" to distinguish it from existing ones, namely the Ovo and the Capuano. During the reign of Robert of Anjou, it became an important cultural centre, attracting writers like Petrarch and Boccaccio.

1 Triumphal Arch
Inspired by Roman antecedents, this arch was completed in 1471 as a commemoration of King Alfonso V of Aragon's conquest of the Kingdom of Naples in 1443.

2 Architecture
In the 15th century five cylindrical towers were added, as was a Catalan courtyard and the Hall of the Barons.

3 Cappella Palatina
The castle's main chapel houses frescoes from the 14th to 16th centuries, as well as a fine Renaissance sculpted tabernacle.

Statues of soldiers on the Triumphal Arch

EAT
Try one of the best sfogliatelle (lovely shell-shaped pastries) at La Sfogliatella Mary, located inside the nearby Galleria Umberto I.

4 Museo Civico
On the first floor are paintings and sculptures, including a 16th-century *Adoration of the Magi* in which the Wise Men are portraits of kings Ferrante I and Alfonso II, and Emperor Charles V. You will also

Cylindrical towers of the Castel Nuovo

can view archaeological excavations through a glass floor. Macabre surprises include skeletons of monks from an early convent on the site.

7 Views

One of the best aspects of a visit to the castle is taking in the magnificent views from its upper walls and terraces. Panoramas include Mount Vesuvius and, on a clear day, even the Sorrentine Peninsula.

FROM FORTRESS TO CIVIC PARK

The castle was once a pioneering work of defensive architecture, with large castellated battlements and a wall with bastions. After Unification, the outer wall was demolished and the area was laid out with lawns and flower gardens, turning the grounds into a space for public enjoyment.

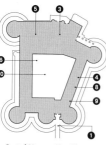

Castel Nuovo Site Plan

find 15th-century bronze doors, depicting royal victories over rebellious barons.

5 Sala dei Baroni

In 1486, Ferrante I of Aragon invited the barons, who were plotting against him, to a ball here, whereupon he had them all executed. Today the hall is notable for its splendid vaults.

6 Excavations

In the left corner of the courtyard, visitors

8 Paintings of Naples

The second floor of the museum focuses on Neapolitan works of a secular nature from the 18th to 20th centuries. Sculptures include *scugnizzi* (street urchins), especially the famous *Fisherboy* by Vincenzo Gemito.

9 Dungeons

Legend has it that prisoners would

regularly disappear from these dungeons without a trace. The cause was discovered to be a huge crocodile that would grab their legs through a drain hole and drag them away.

10 Inner Courtyard

This space has typically Catalan features, such as the "depressed" arches – broader and flatter than Italian types – and an external grand staircase.

Inside the Cappella Palatina

DUOMO

◉ P1 ⌂ Via Duomo 147 ☏ 081 44 90 97 ⌚ 8:30am–1:30pm & 2:30–7:30pm Mon–Sat, 8am–1pm & 4:30–7:30pm Sun

Naples' Gothic cathedral was originally built in the 13th century, but a patchwork of improvements and renovations have turned it into the lively fusion of architectural styles we see today. One of the Duomo's chapels is dedicated to the city's patron saint, San Gennaro; the Museum of the Treasure of San Gennaro is next to the building.

Main entrance to the cathedral

1 Façade and Portals

The Neo-Gothic façade of Naples' cathedral was restored in the early 20th century, but it is still graced with three original portals dating back to the 1400s.

2 Interior and Ceiling

The interior of the cathedral never fails to dazzle visitors. The floorplan is 100-m-(330-ft-) long, with a nave and two aisles lined with chapels. Sixteen pillars support arches that are flanked by granite columns.

3 Font

The main baptismal font lies to the left of the nave. The Egyptian basalt basin is of Hellenistic origin and the Baroque upper part, which is made from bronze and marble, dates back to 1618.

4 Cappella di San Gennaro

⌚ 9:30am–5pm Mon–Sat, 9:30am–1:30pm Sun & public hols (book online in advance) 🌐 cappellasangennaro.it ⌨

This Baroque extravaganza to the centre-right of the nave was built in the 1600s using marble and precious metals. Great artists of the day decorated its walls and domed ceiling.

5 Relics

The main reliquary is in Cappella di San Gennaro; it has a gold bust of San Gennaro containing his skull bones. You will also find a vial with ampoules of his blood.

6 Crypt of the Succorpo

The style and complexity of this 15th-century chapel have led some scholars to attribute the design to leading Renaissance architect Donato Bramante.

7 Cappella Capece Minutolo

Considered to be one of the best-preserved examples of the Gothic style of the 13th and 14th centuries, this chapel has a beautiful mosaic floor and striking altar frescoes.

Stunning detail on the ceiling of the Cappella di San Gennaro

The Museum of the Treasure of San Gennaro

8 Museum of the Treasure of San Gennaro

🕙 9:30am–6pm daily (last entry 5pm) 🌐 tesorosan gennaro.it ⭐

This museum features jewellery, reliquaries, paintings, sculptures and much more. Among the items on display is the stunning jewelled Mitre of San Gennaro, which weighs 18 kgs (40 lbs) and is made from 3,694 precious stones (198 emeralds, 168 rubies and 3,328 diamonds).

9 Santa Restituta

Naples' oldest structure, Santa Restituta was commissioned in the 4th century by Emperor Constantine, who made Christianity the official religion of the Roman Empire. Inside the basilica, which is dedicated to St Restituta, an early Christian martyr, are a magnificent Romanesque fresco and mosaics dating back to 1322.

10 Baptistry

This is the oldest baptistry in the western world. It was built by the end of the 4th century and is decorated with splendid mosaics. The sunken font is thought to have come from an ancient temple that was devoted to the Greek god Dionysus.

SAN GENNARO

Naples' patron saint, San Gennaro opposed the Roman Emperor Diocletian's campaign of persecution against Christians by hiding the believers of this faith. Eventually he was arrested and then beheaded in 305 CE. According to legend, his blood was collected by a pious nurse, Eusebia, and preserved in the Catacombs of San Gennaro (p66). A believer is said to have discovered that the dried blood liquefied on demand, and by the 14th century this miracle had inspired a city-wide cult.

MUSEO ARCHEOLOGICO NAZIONALE

📍 N1 🏛 Piazza Museo 18/19 🕐 9am–7:30pm Wed–Mon (ticket office closes 6:30pm) 🌐 mann-napoli.it ↗

Among the world's top museums of ancient art, the National Archaeological Museum of Naples overwhelms with its wealth of artifacts. It was built in the 16th century as headquarters for the royal cavalry and was later turned into a museum for finds that were unearthed at Pompeii and Herculaneum. The museum is home to much of the Farnese Collection of important ancient treasures.

1 Pottery and Metal Vessels

Pottery here includes Greek and Etruscan *kraters*, Roman terracotta jars, vases and figurines. Grecian urns, with red figures on black backgrounds, depict a variety of scenes.

2 Marble Sculpture

Replicas of some of the most renowned ancient Classical sculptures by artists such as Phidias, Lysippus, Praxiteles and Polyclitus are housed here, along with striking Greek and Roman busts.

TOP TIP

Maps can be found at the info point to the left of the main entrance.

3 Il Gabinetto Segreto

Also known as the "Secret Room", this collection has erotic art from Pompeii and Herculaneum. The contents caused a scandal on first opening, and the displays have often been censored.

4 Mosaics

Small chips of coloured glass and stone (*tesserae*) were used to create colourful mosaics for display in wealthy homes and public buildings.

5 Glass and Stone Vessels

Masters at producing coloured and transparent glassware, the Romans

Clockwise from top left
An array of classic sculptures; polychrome terracotta vase; gold ducat; Roman mosaic from Pompeii's House of the Faun

pioneered new artisanal techniques. Highlights of the collection include the celebrated Farnese Cup, engraved in semi-precious stone with layers of agate and sardonyx, and the blue vase. Used as a wine vessel, the vase was discovered in a Pompeii tomb.

6 Friezes, Frescoes and Murals

These striking Roman works were excavated from Pompeii and disclose a great deal about the nature of society and religion of the time.

7 Weapons, Jewellery and Domestic Items

Shields, helmets and swords remind us of combat, but metalsmiths also made

Admiring the ceiling fresco by Pietro Bardellino

decorative pieces. Domestic items include lamps and cups.

8 Egyptian and Prehistoric Items

This collection, housed in the museum's basement, showcases art from the Ancient Kingdom (2700–2200 BCE) to the Roman age. Funereal sarcophagi and mummies – including one of a crocodile – can be seen here.

9 Incised Gems, Coins and Epigraphs

The collection of incised gems contains Greek and Roman pieces, with bronze, silver and gold coins, including some from Magna Graecia. Ancient records include the *Tavole di Eraclea* (3rd century BCE).

10 Bronze Sculpture

Bronze masterpieces that once decorated

the Villa dei Papiri in Herculaneum, including a resting Hermes, a number of fauns and water-bearers are among the many statues on display here.

Individual Masterpieces

1. Farnese Hercules
Created and signed by the great Glykon of Athens, this marble sculpture, on the museum's ground floor, is a copy and enlargement of a lost bronze original by the 4th-century BCE Greek master Lysippus. It was discovered in the ruins of the Baths of Caracalla in Rome, where it is considered to have served as a magnificent decoration for the imperial pleasure dome. The work is a depiction of the mythical hero at rest, exhausted after having completed his round of 12 super-human tasks.

Mosaic depicting Alexander the Great on horseback

2. Farnese Bull
Found in the Baths of Caracalla in Rome during excavations, this is the largest sculptural group to have survived from antiquity to date. On display on the ground floor, it is one of the best-known pieces in the Farnese Collection. It recounts the story of Dirce (the first wife of Lykos, King of Thebes), who treated Antiope poorly and is being punished by the latter's sons by being tied to a bull. It is probably a copy – though some claim it may be the original – of a 2nd-century BCE Greek work and is Hellenistic.

3. The Doryphoros
On display on the ground floor, this is the most complete replica of the celebrated Doryphoros, created in about 440 BCE by Polyclitus of Argos and widely regarded as one of the finest Greek sculptures ever made. The name means "spear-bearer" and one can see that the figure once held a spear in his left hand. It is thought to represent Achilles, and the statue was known in ancient times as the Canon, exhibiting perfect proportions in every aspect of its depiction of the human form. The sculptor developed a complex theory of measurements, related to music, for the ideal construction of the human body.

4. Farnese Cup
The star of the museum's cameo and incised gem collection on the ground floor is this glistening masterpiece, carved from a single piece of stone, specifically chosen by the artist for its layering of agate and sardonyx. The outer face of the cup has an image of Medusa; inside is an allegorical scene that probably alludes to the fertility of the Nile.

The remarkable Farnese Bull marble sculpture

The cup was produced in Egypt in the 2nd or 1st century BCE.

5. Alexander the Great Mosaic

Found as a floor decoration in Pompeii's House of the Faun, a grand aristocratic mansion of the 2nd century BCE, this Hellenistic mosaic, on display on the first floor, is certainly one of the most elegant and exciting to have survived. The subject is the routing of Darius's Persian armies by Alexander the Great's cavalry. The monumentality of the work is impressive and it is almost certainly a copy of a lost painting of great importance, possibly by Philoxenos. Fragmentary as it is, there are still some one million *tesserae* (tiles) in its composition.

6. Dancing Faun

A more joyous image of freedom and exuberant health would be hard to imagine. This bronze on the first floor was found in Pompeii's House of the Faun, to which it gives its name, as a decoration in the atrium to greet arriving guests. Two ancient replicas of this Hellenistic figure are known to exist, so it must have been a popular and inspiring object.

7. Hermes at Rest

Were it not for the wings on his feet, one might suppose that this bronze Hermes (Mercury) was just a young athlete taking a break from his exertions rather than a god. The proportions of this sculpture were inspired by the work of Lysippus. It can be viewed on the second floor.

8. Sleeping and Drunken Satyrs

Satyrs to the ancients were always a symbol of pure hedonism – not just sexual licence, but every form of ease and indulgence. Located on the second floor, these two figures from the Villa dei Papiri (*p40*) express a light-hearted indolence that is as implicitly erotic as it is earthy. The ancients believed

that physical pleasure and delight were part of man's divine essence and gifts from the gods.

9. Sacrifice of Iphigenia

Found in Pompeii, in the so-called House of the Tragic Poet, this painting shows the dramatic moment when the sacrifice of Iphigenia is halted by the intervention of Artemis (Diana), who kills a deer instead. The fresco was once considered a faithful copy of a painting by the Greek artist Timante, but it is now thought to be an original Roman depiction, due primarily to its overall lack of compositional unity. The painting is found on the second floor of the museum, though it's sometimes loaned to other galleries.

10. Achilles and Chiron

Retrieved from the so-called Basilica in Herculaneum, this fresco on the second floor depicts Achilles, the young hero of the Trojan War with his mentor, the centaur Chiron. Since this large work was originally crafted as decoration for a public building, the message is clear – heed the elemental forces of Nature (symbolized by the centaur) to find balance and fulfilment in life. The image is based on a famous sculptural group, probably Greek, now lost but known to have stood in ancient Rome, as recorded by Pliny the Elder.

Fresco showing the sacrifice of Iphigenia

MUSEO DI CAPODIMONTE

📍 K1 🚪 Porta Grande Via Capodimonte; Porta Piccola Via Miano 2
🕐 First floor: 8:30am–7:30pm Thu–Tue (ticket desk closes 6:30pm);
Second floor: 8:30am–5pm Mon–Sat 🌐 capodimonte.cultura.gov.it 🔗

A palace, museum and porcelain factory, the Capodimonte has housed a large and celebrated part of the Farnese Collection since 1759. The building was formerly the property of the House of Savoy and the residence of the Dukes of Aosta until 1947. Today, the museum is prized for its collection, with a vast permanent exhibition featuring European art from the 14th to the 17th centuries. Caravaggio's *Flagellation of Christ* is a particular highlight.

Painting of Saint Louis of Toulouse (c 1317)

3 16th-Century Art
Here you'll find a serene *Assumption of the Virgin* by Pinturicchio, an *Assumption* by Fra Bartolomeo and works by Titian and Raphael.

4 17th-Century Art
Caravaggio's *Flagellation of Christ* and Artemisia Gentileschi's graphic *Judith Slaying Holofernes* are impressive.

TOP TIP

Entry to the museum is free on the first Sunday of every month.

5 18th-Century Art
Neapolitan artist Francesco Solimena is well represented here. Look out for his opulent

1 Pre-14th- and 14th-Century Art
Most of the earliest Italian art in the museum was acquired in the 19th and 20th centuries. Important works include Simone Martini's lavish Gothic masterpiece *San Ludovico di Tolosa*.

2 15th-Century Art
Some powerful works here include Botticelli's *Madonna with Child and Angels* and Bellini's sublime *Transfiguration*.

The ballroom in the Reggia di Capodimonte

portrait of a prince, Principe Tarsia Spinelli. Other canvases provide historical views of the Bay of Naples.

6 19th-Century and Modern Art

Paintings of moments past and landscapes dominate this part of the collection. Endearing are the sculptures of street urchins by Vincenzo Gemito, but the signature modern work is Andy Warhol's garish *Vesuvius*.

7 Porcelain Parlour

Designed for Queen Maria Amalia, this parlour is home to painted and gilded porcelain used to form figurative scenes.

8 Drawings

Sketches and studies by great artists are on display here, including several works by Fra' Bartolomeo, Raphael and Michelangelo. Open mornings only.

9 Decorative Arts

The palace is filled with countless examples of the decorative arts. Its rich collection features many items such as ivory carvings, Roman sculptures and tapestries, along with exquisite 18th- and 19th-century furniture pieces housed in the palace rooms.

10 Ballroom

Initially conceived as a hunting lodge, the palace later grew into a grand three-storey property with an expansive ballroom for entertaining.

ROYAL PORCELAIN FACTORY

Charles of Bourbon established the Reale Fabbrica delle Porcellane in 1743 and it quickly became celebrated for the refinement of its porcelain creations. The factory flourished until 1759, when the king returned to his native Spain and took its staff with him, but it reopened in 1771, and production of top-quality pieces recommenced. The mark for objects made here was generally a crowned "N" in blue on the underside.

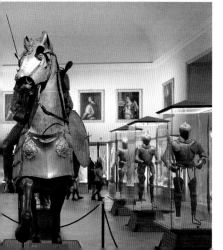

Armour-clad knight on horseback

CERTOSA E MUSEO DI SAN MARTINO

📍 L4 🏛 Largo San Martino 5 📞 081 229 45 03 🕐 8:30am–7:30pm Thu–Tue 📶

Naples seems to disappear as you enter this vast and beautiful monastery, built in 1325 by Charles, Duke of Calabria in a spot overlooking the entire city. The layout of the place, ensconced just below the massive Castel Sant' Elmo, is palatial, with two cloisters and a museum and gallery housed inside.

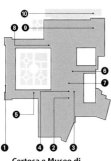

Certosa e Museo di San Martino Site Plan

1 Façade
Initially built in Gothic style, the façade has been overlain with refined Baroque decorations, like the large windows.

2 Choir and Sacristy
The richly carved walnut choir stalls were executed between 1629 and 1631 by Orazio de Orio and Giovanni Mazzuoli. The cherubs and the abundance of volute curves are lovely.

3 Church
The elaborate nave of the church is a display of Baroque art and decoration, offering a lively snapshot of Neapolitan religious art from the 17th and 18th centuries crowded into a single space.

EAT
The best place for a meal in the area is Renzo e Lucia (renzoe lucianapoli.it). Sat atop Vomero hill, it offers a great view.

4 Sculpture and Marble Decor
Italian painter Francesco Solimena designed the altar, which has silvered papier-mâché putti by Giacomo Colombo.

5 Chiostro Grande
With a 64-marble-columned portico, the

Colonnaded path leading to the Chiostro Grande

Bust of Saint Bruno at Chiostro Grande

the main part of the church. All of them are rich with brightly coloured marble and opulent gilded stucco trim.

7 Paintings and Frescoes

Dominating the ceiling is the beautiful *Ascension of Jesus* fresco by Lanfranco, while the counter-façade has the lovely *Pietà* by Stanzione.

8 Quarto del Priore

🕘 9:40am–7pm Thu–Tue

These were the quarters of the monastery's Prior, spiritual leader and the only one of the monks who was allowed contact with the outside world. Aristocratic furnishings and priceless works of art from the Certosa collection adorn the monastery walls.

9 Naval Section

This section commemorates the Bourbon army and showcases royal barges, weapons and model frigates.

10 Gardens and Belvederes

The views from the Certosa are picture-perfect, and the gardens are lush and fragrant.

Large Cloister was designed by Giovanni Antonio Dosio. Cosimo Fanzago's marble masterpiece and sculpted skulls at the monks' cemetery are highlights.

6 Chapels and Subsidiary Rooms

The eight chapels are decorated in a unified style consistent with

THE MONASTERY'S GUARDIAN

Before entering the Certosa, take in the castle hovering above it. The monastery was built directly beneath Castel Sant'Elmo for the protection that it afforded. The original structure dates from Angevin times, but it was rebuilt by the Spanish in the 16th century on a six-pointed star design. Its original name was Sant'Erasmo, after the hill it stands on, but the name became corrupted over the centuries, first to Sant'Eramo, then Sant'Ermo and finally to Sant'Elmo.

Impressive interior of the church

Museum Exhibits

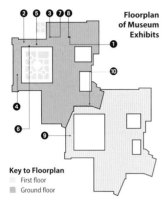

Floorplan of Museum Exhibits

Key to Floorplan
▒ First floor
▓ Ground floor

1. High Renaissance Art
The most significant works here are marble sculptures, including a late 16th-century work by Pietro Bernini, *Madonna with Child and St John the Baptist as a Child*. Its twisting composition, with St John kissing the Child's foot and Mary looking on, embodies tenderness.

2. Early Italian Renaissance Art
Of special note here is a 15th-century view of Naples, the *Tavola Strozzi*, by an unknown artist. It is also the first painted view of the city from the sea.

3. Early International Renaissance Art
The most outstanding piece here is a triptych by Jean Bourdichon of the Virgin and Child and saints John the Baptist and John the Evangelist (c 1414). The work employs masterful perspective and anatomical detail.

4. Baroque Art
This era is the collection's strongest suit. Significant sculptures include a *Veiled Christ* in terracotta by Corradini. A devout Lanfranco painting, *Madonna with Child and Saints Domenico and Gennaro*, is typical of the age.

5. Jusepe de Ribera
The great Spanish artist, who worked in Naples for most of his

Beautiful triptych by Jean Bourdichon

St Sebastian Tended by the Holy Women by Jusepe de Ribera

life, was appreciated for his dramatic style. His *St Sebastian* is one of the most powerful works, showing the ecstatic face of the young man, his body pierced with arrows.

6. Micco Spadaro
This artist's *Martyrdom of St Sebastian* provides an interesting contrast with Ribera's work. Rather than focusing on the man in close-up, it shows him off to the right being tied up, just before Roman soldiers let their arrows fly. Another Spadaro work shows the monks of the Certosa thanking Christ for sparing them from the plague, with a view of Naples' bay through the arcades.

7. Stanzione
Stanzione's *Baptism of Christ* is worth noting for the luminous way the flesh is rendered. He achieved this through the strategic use of *chiaroscuro* (light and shade).

8. Nativity Collection
Of all the priceless nativity scenes and figures here, the *Cuciniello Presepe* is by far the most elaborate. The manger scene is quite lost amid 180 shepherds, 10 horses, 8 dogs, folk going about their business, a Moroccan musical ensemble and much more. Lighting effects create dawn, day, dusk and night.

9. Glass, Porcelain and Gold
The objects here go back to the 1500s and include painted plates, vases, tiles, pitchers, mirrors and figurines. Subject matter ranges from religious themes, such as a coral and gold Crucifix, to humdrum scenes from daily life.

10. Neapolitan 19th-Century Art
Pre- and post-Unification was a time when Italians awoke to their national heritage and began to sculpt an identity through their art. City views and its environs are informative of bygone days, as are the wonderful portraits.

NATIVITY SCENES
When exploring Naples, you'll no doubt encounter a number of elaborately crafted, miniature nativity scenes, both in museums and at street stall and markets. Called *presepe*, derived from the Latin *praesepe* or "feeding trough", referring to the Christ Child's initial resting place, the art of the nativity scene in southern Italy grew to become a major undertaking in the 1600s. Kings and queens would vie with each other to gather the most impressive, dazzling, poignant and often humorous display, commissioning the best artists and designers of the day. It was not until the end of the 19th century that these wonderful works were fully recognized as an artistic genre in their own right.

The oldest example of a monumental Neapolitan *presepe* comes from the church of San Giovanni a Carbonara; sculpted by Pietro and Giovanni Alemanno in 1478–84, it originally included 41 life-size wooden figures, of which 19 still survive in the church. Today, the craft remains very much alive, though talented artisans now craft *pastori*: secular and defiantly modern scenes and figures, including local pop stars and politicians.

POMPEII

🗺 E4 ⧉ Via Villa dei Misteri 2 🕐 Apr–Oct: 9am–7pm daily; Nov–Mar: 9am–5pm daily (last entry 90 mins before closing time) 🌐 pompeiisites.org ♿

Since the devastating eruption of Vesuvius in 79 CE, Pompeii has been a Roman city eerily preserved in time. Most of the city's grand buildings were perfectly preserved by volcanic ash. The result is a uniquely evocative ancient site that has fascinated visitors since its discovery in the 18th century.

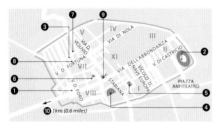

name of this house, which covered an entire city block. Wall decorations and *opus sectile* mosaic marble floors can be seen here.

Statue of a dancing faun, House of the Faun

1 Forum
Every Roman city centred commercial, civic, political and religious life around the Forum, generally a long rectangular area.

2 Amphitheatre
Far to the east stands Pompeii's amphitheatre – a typical oval shape, though small by Roman standards. It was the first of its kind to be built for gladiatorial combat.

3 House of the Faun
The 1-m (3-ft) bronze statue of the Dancing Faun, found here in the middle of the small courtyard pond, accounts for the

4 Theatre
The large theatre, built in the 2nd century BCE in a Greek style, used the slope of the land for the *cavea* (seating area).

5 House of Menander
This grand house includes an atrium, peristyle and baths. It proved to be a treasure-trove of silver objects, now on display in Naples' Museo Archeologico.

6 Brothel
The *lupanarium*, the largest of the ruined Roman city's brothels, has frescoes depicting erotic, sometimes explicit, acts, which

The Forum with Mount Vesuvius rising behind

 DRINK
Chora Café
(chorapompei.com),
a beloved local spot,
is the perfect place
to stop for refresh-
ments as you explore
the ancient city.

informed the clients what services the sex-workers would provide.

7 House of the Vettii

One of the most beautiful houses in Pompeii, this house has splendid paintings and friezes featuring mythological themes.

8 House of the Golden Cupids

This sumptuous house was named after the gold-leaf decorations of *amorini* (cupids) in the bedroom. It was owned by the Poppaea family, that of Nero's second wife. The gardens were adorned with sculptures, marble tables and a pool.

9 Stabian Baths

To the west of Via Stabiana are the 4th-century BCE Stabian Baths. These baths were heated using an innovative system that circulated hot air through the walls.

10 Via dei Sepolcri

This "street of tombs", flanked by burial sites, commercial buildings and villas, lies outside the city gates, for fear of bad luck.

CURRENT EXCAVATIONS

With excavation work underway in Pompeii, archaeologists keep uncovering treasures. A finely preserved chariot, likely used for festivals, was discovered in 2021. In 2023, a fresco depicting the likely predecessor to pizza was found. It is estimated that over a third of the city is still to be uncovered, with excavations ongoing.

Wall decoration in the House of the Vettii

Herculaneum, Oplontis and Stabiae

1. Villa dei Papyri
The remains of the resort town of Herculaneum were discovered before Pompeii but were harder to excavate since they were covered by a thicker layer of volcanic ash. Fortunately, this also meant that every aspect was better preserved. This villa was one of the first to be explored, housing art treasures now in the Museo Archeologico (p28). The papyrus scrolls that give the villa its name are in the National Library.

2. House of the Stags
The name derives from the sculpture of stags being attacked by dogs that was found here. Other sculptures include a Satyr with Wineskin and a Drunken Hercules.

3. House of the Mosaic Atrium
This house takes its name from its mosaic floor of black-and-white geometric patterns. Gardens and rooms with views of the sea must have made it a lovely place to relax.

4. Trellis House
A wonderfully preserved example of what an ordinary multi-family dwelling was like, this building is two storeys high. It has a balcony that overhangs the pavement and its walls are composed of wood and reed laths with crude tufa and lime masonry to fill in the frame.

5. House of Neptune and Amphitrite
This is named after the mosaic of the sea god and his nymph-bride that adorns the fountain in the summer dining room at the back of the house.

Fresco in the College of the Augustales, Herculaneum

Mosaic at the House of Neptune and Amphitrite

Other fine mosaics can be seen here too. The shop attached to the house has wooden structures and furniture in perfect condition.

6. Suburban Baths

Built in 10 BCE, these traditional baths are fascinating. They are divided into male and female sections, both decorated with the same sea-themed mosaics featuring tritons and fish. At the centre of the complex is an open porticoed area used as a gymnasium.

7. Thermopolia

The Thermopolia is an example of a fast-food outlet of the day. The terracotta amphorae set into the marble counter top would have contained various comestibles. Only wealthy people had facilities to cook food, so most would stop by such a place to eat.

8. House of the Wooden Partition

This house was discovered with its wooden partition perfectly intact. A kind of "accordion" partition was devised here to separate the atrium from the *tablinum*, the room of business affairs.

9. Villas of Oplontis

The beautifully preserved aristocratic villas of Poppaea Sabina and Crassus, who were buried during the eruption of Vesuvius, are located in what was once the ancient resort of Oplontis. The complex includes gardens, porticoes, private baths, a pool and astounding wall decorations.

10. Villas of Stabiae

Set on the Varano Hill just outside Castellammare di Stabia, two villas preserve mosaic floors, gardens, peristyles and frescoes. Villa Arianna is named after a fresco of Ariadne being abandoned by Theseus. Villa San Marco sports a gymnasium, pool and interesting frescoes.

THE ERUPTION OF 79 CE

On 24 August 79 CE, Mount Vesuvius suddenly erupted. The apex of the calamity started at about 10am and by 1pm it was all over – nearby towns on the mountain slopes like Herculaneum, Oplontis and Stabiae were covered with lava, and Pompeii and its citizens were entirely buried. It lay undiscovered until 1750.

Pliny the Younger survived to write an eyewitness account of the events: "On Mount Vesuvius broad sheets of fire and leaping flames blazed at several points, their bright glare emphasized by the darkness… an ominous thick smoke, spreading over the earth like a flood, enveloping the earth in night… earth-shocks so violent it seemed the world was being turned upside down… the shrill cries of women, the wailing of children, the shouting of men… Many lifted up their hands to the gods, but a great number believed there were no gods, and that this was to be the world's last, eternal night…The flames and smell of sulphur… heralded the approaching fire… The dense fumes… choked… nearly everyone, to death."

Colourful houses and boats at Marina Grande

CAPRI

C5 Piazza Umberto I; capritourism.com

Ever since ancient times, this saddle-shaped rock in the Bay of Naples has attracted illustrious visitors, including Roman emperors, princes, politicians and poets, all drawn by the idea of the good life. The island does have something special, perhaps generated by its sheer dramatic beauty, its crystal-clear waters and its lush vineyards and lemon and olive groves.

1 Marina Grande
Whether by ferry, hydrofoil or private yacht, virtually all visitors to the island arrive at this little port town – a mesmerizing sight as you approach. Despite the bustle, the town is just as laidback as the rest of Capri and is home to the island's biggest beach.

2 Capri Town
Piazza Umberto I, which is known simply as the "Piazzetta", is the town's outdoor salon, featuring chic bars and restaurants. It is especially lively in the evenings.

3 Villa Jovis
Emperor Tiberius's 1st-century-CE villa, built on the cliff's edge, is now in ruins. The views of the Bay of Naples, from the highest point at this end of the island, are dazzling.

4 Arco Naturale
Follow signs from Capri Town for this easy-going walking trail, where rocky staircases offer fine panoramas of the mainland coastline. The Natural Arch itself

> **TRANSPORT**
> Ferries and hydrofoils leave from many ports, including Mergellina and Molo Beverello in Naples, Sorrento, Positano, Amalfi, Salerno, Ischia and Castellammare di Stabia.

consists of a huge limestone crag, jutting out with the bright turquoise sea seen below.

5 Via Krupp and Faraglioni
Via Krupp is a switchback path carved into the cliff face. From here there are views of Faraglioni rocks.

6 Marina Piccola
This small harbour has private bathing huts, a pebbly arc of beach, wonderful rocks for diving from and several good fish restaurants.

7 Monte Solaro
No trip to the island is complete without a chair-lift ride up to Capri's highest peak, from which

you can look down on the pastoral timelessness of lemon groves, little white houses and endless flower gardens that cover the island – breathtaking.

8 Anacapri and Punta Carena

Before 1877, when the road was built, Anacapri was isolated and is still less pretentious than the rest of the island. From here, another great jaunt is to the lighthouse at Punta Carena, where a rocky beach, as well as good facilities and restaurants awaits.

9 Villa San Michele

Built by a Swedish doctor on the site of one of Tiberius's houses, Villa San Michele is an eclectic mix of Romanesque, Renaissance and Moorish styles, surrounded by gorgeous gardens.

10 Blue Grotto

This sea cave with crystalline blue water creates eye-catching silver reflections. Local boats ferry visitors inside – be aware that the grotto can close at short notice due to tide levels.

Clockwise from right
Stunning switchbacks of Via Krupp; Blue Grotto illuminated by an otherworldly blue light; Capri's bustling Piazzetta; scenic view from Monte Solaro

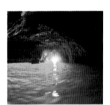

AMALFI, RAVELLO AND POSITANO

☉ E5

With its dramatic coastline dotted with clifftop villages, the beautiful Amalfi Coast has been luring travellers since ancient times. The town of Amalfi is tucked between mountains and sea, Positano is famous for its pastel-hued homes, while Ravello sits dramatically atop a rocky spur.

Enjoying the view from Villa Rufolo

1 Museo della Carta, Amalfi

Discover Amalfi's role in the history of paper-making at this small museum (p55), which is evocatively set in a historical paper mill.

2 Duomo di Amalfi

☐ Piazza Duomo
⊙ 9am–7:45pm daily
ⓦ museodiocesano amalfi.it **☉**

Sitting atop a staircase, Amalfi's cathedral is dedicated to St Andrew and features the 13th-century Cloister of Paradise, museum, crypt and sumptuous Baroque interior.

VIEW
From the garden of Villa Rufolo in Ravello, you can see the whole of the coast stretching away into the distance.

ouses of Positano overlooking Fornillo Beach

There's an extra fee for the museum and cloister.

3 Valle delle Ferriere, Amalfi

Hike from Amalfi into the Valle delle Ferriere (Valley of the Mills), where ruins of once prosperous paper mills are surrounded by a lush forest.

4 Atrani

Amalfi's next-door neighbour to the east is the fishing village of Atrani, which is one of Italy's smallest municipalities. The narrow alleys and main square preserve its historic character, which was used to beautiful effect in the Netflix series *Ripley* (2024).

5 Villa Cimbrone, Ravello

The creation of an English lord, Ernest Beckett, the house (now a hotel) imitates the Moorish style, while its gardens feature Classical temples.

6 Villa Rufolo, Ravello

This 800-year-old Arab-style palace and its terraced gardens have inspired many visitors. The terrace is used in summer for staging concerts.

7 Duomo di Ravello

- 📍 Piazza del Duomo
- 🕐 9am–7pm daily
- 🌐 chiesaravello.com

The 11th-century cathedral is a treasure-trove of works. Its beautiful pulpit (1272) has twisted columns resting on sculpted lions at the base.

8 Scala

This tiny hamlet, built on a succession of terraces, is well worth a visit for the outstanding views it affords when you look back at its larger neighbour, Ravello.

9 Church of Santa Maria Assunta, Positano

- 📍 Piazza Flavio Gioia
- 📞 089 87 54 80
- 🕐 9:30am–noon & 4–8pm daily

With its multicoloured dome and Baroque interior, Positano's church is as pretty as its setting.

10 Fornillo Beach, Positano

Follow the scenic pathway hugging the cliff to this beautiful beach set in a cove flanked by two watchtowers; the perfect respite from the summer crowds.

RAVELLO MUSIC FESTIVAL

Each summer Ravello is transformed into a haven for music lovers. Its famous music festival *(ravello festival.com)*, featuring chamber music, opera, dance and jazz, was inspired by Richard Wagner and Edvard Grieg, the 19th-century composers, who were moved by the natural beauty of Ravello. For the most part, concerts and events take place at Villa Rufolo and the Auditorium Oscar Niemeyer.

PAESTUM

📍 H6 🏛 Via Magna Graecia 919 (SS18) 🕐 8:30am–7:30pm daily 🔗

This atmospheric site recalls the days when the Greeks governed this region, which was part of a rich colony they called Magna Graecia. The beautifully prepared Doric temples here have stood for over 2,000 years and are a testament to the ancient people who built them.

TRANSPORT
Frequent buses run from Salerno to Paestum (*fsbusitalia campania.it*). You can also catch the train to Paestum station, near the site, from Naples.

1 Walls
At its peak, the ancient town of Paestum was large and prosperous, as evidenced by its impressive 5 km (3 miles) of walls, set off with towers and gates at strategic points.

2 Temple of Hera
The oldest temple on the grounds, from c 530 BCE, was most likely dedicated to two deities, Hera and Zeus.

3 Temple of "Neptune"
The last of the three temples to be built at Paestum, in about 450 BCE, is also the finest and the best preserved. It may have been dedicated to Neptune (Poseidon), but some scholars argue for Apollo, and others for Zeus.

4 Amphitheatre
This Roman structure dates from the 1st century BCE

Impressive ruins of Greek temples, Paestum

6 Museum
🕘 9am–7:30pm Tue–Sun 🌐 museo paestum.cultura.gov.it

This informative museum exhibits finds from Paestum and several important sites nearby. One of those sites is the Sanctuary of Hera Argiva, built by the Greeks at the mouth of the River Sele in about 600 BCE. There is also a collection of Roman finds upstairs.

7 Tomb Frescoes
Most famous of the exhibits in the museum are the tomb frescoes. Virtually the only examples of ancient Greek painting to survive, they are full of light and bright colours.

8 Sculpture
Prime examples in this category of the museum include archaic metopes (decorative architectural elements) and one of two dancing girls from the Sanctuary of Hera Argiva, so well carved in bas-relief that each of the figures seems to be moving in space.

MAGNA GRAECIA
Being great seafarers, the ancient Greeks were indefatigable colonizers. Each important city-state sent out expeditions all over the Mediterranean to set up new cities. Paestum (Poseidonia) was one such Greek city, as were Naples (Neapolis), Cumae and many more.

9 Pottery
Fine examples of Grecian urns are on view, including a *krater* with red-figured painting on black, depicting a young satyr and a girl reluctant to succumb to his blandishments, and an amphora with black figures on red celebrating the fruit of the vine.

10 Artifacts
Other artifacts here include a bronze vase that contained honey. Amazingly, it was still liquid at the time it was found due to unique atmospheric conditions below ground.

Bust on display in the museum

or later, and is only partially excavated. The rest lies under the 18th-century road, but some of the exposed part has been rebuilt. Its capacity was small – only about 2,000 – compared to others in the region.

5 Temple of "Ceres"
Votive offerings found here suggest that this small temple, located further north than the other sites, was dedicated to the goddess Athena.

Ancient tomb frescoes in the museum

TOP 10 OF EVERYTHING

Painted tiles for sale in Naples

ANCIENT SITES

1 Pompeii
There are few ancient centres as evocative as Pompeii (p38). Hauntingly preserved under Mount Vesuvius's volcanic ash, the ruined city offers a vivid snapshot of ancient Rome at its peak. The vast city's brothels, baths, bars, private dwellings and civic buildings speak of normal, albeit affluent, life over a thousand years ago.

2 Herculaneum
This ancient seaside resort (p100) was buried under layers of ash following the eruption of Vesuvius. Better preserved than Pompeii, the site houses two-storey homes with their internal architecture and décor intact. No expense was spared in making these luxury homes shine.

3 Villas of Oplontis, Torre Annunziata
Oplontis (p101) was an elite seaside town destroyed and preserved by the eruption. The Villa of Poppaea Sabina is a luxurious residential complex with frescoes, a pool, baths and gardens, while the nearby Villa of Lucius Crassius Tertius was an important distribution centre for local produce.

4 Villas of Stabiae, Castellammare di Stabia
The ancient city of Stabiae (p41) has some of the best examples of Roman seaside villas. Villa Arianna has elegant mosaic flooring with black-and-white decorative motifs and fine frescoes depicting mythological themes. The colonnaded atrium at Villa San Marco is particularly impressive.

5 Paestum
 H6 Via Magna Graecia, 919 8:30am–5pm daily (Apr–Oct: to 7pm) museopaestum.cultura.gov.it
Long before the territory-hungry Romans made their mark in southern

The well-preserved Greek Temple of Hera at Paestum

Italy, the Greeks were thriving. Paestum, a major ancient city on the coast of the Tyrrhenian Sea, contains the ruins of some of Greece's most important temples, as well as a later Roman amphitheatre. In the iconic Tomb of the Diver, you'll find a fresco (500–475 BCE) depicting a naked boy diving from a tower into a pool of water.

6 Villa Jovis, Capri
 C5 Via Tiberio, 80073 Capri 10am–4pm daily
The ruins of Emperor Tiberius I's villa, built in the 1st century BCE, perch on a cliff edge, offering sublime views of the Bay of Naples. The villa is accessible via a 45-minute uphill walk, and you can stop off en route at the Parco Astarita terrace to snap a shot of the Gulf of Salerno, Naples and Sorrento. For something a little less charming, the Tiberius's Leap cliff drop is where the emperor is said to have hurled enemies and servants to their death.

7 Parco Sommerso di Baia, Bacoli

📍 B4 📍 Via Lucullo, 94, 80070 Bacoli
🕐 9am–7pm daily 🌐 subaia.com/en/snorheling-baia ♿

Known as the "submerged Pompeii", the remains of this ancient Roman port are buried under water thanks to the region's volatile geology. Accessible via diving and boat tours, the underwater park is part of a protected marine area, with the city's mosaics and sculptures now frequented by an abundance of aquatic life.

8 Amphitheatre of Capua, Santa Maria Capua Vetere

📍 C1 📍 Via Roberto d'Angiò, 48, 81055 Santa Maria Capua Vetere
🕐 9am–4pm daily ♿

Possibly the first ever Roman amphitheatre and second only in size to the Colosseum in Rome, this was home to the first gladiator school. The site was also the starting point of the third slave rebellion against the Roman Republic, led by Spartacus. Here, you can find the Museum of the Gladiators.

9 Catacombs of San Gennaro, Naples

Stretching beneath the streets of Naples is this paleo-Christian burial and worship site *(p66)*, spread across two levels and dating to the 2nd century CE. It was likely the tomb of a noble family, with spaces for other members of the Christian community. Look out for the eerie fresco depicting the family of Theotecnus.

10 Parco Archeologico del Pausilypon

📍 J2 📍 Discesa Coroglio 36
🕐 9am–1.30pm Tue–Sun ♿

This Roman seaside villa and amphitheatre were built in the 1st century BCE. They are accessed via the Seiano Grotto, a Roman-era tunnel carved deep into the hillside. The villa was built by the knight Publio Vedio Pollio; after his death in 15 BCE, it fell into the hands of Emperor Augustus.

TOP 10
FRESCOES UNEARTHED AT POMPEII

1. Leda and the Swan
Depicting the story of Zeus who turned into a swan to seduce Leda, this fresco is beautifully preserved.

2. Priapus
This fresco shows Priapus, the god of fertility, balancing his genitals with a bag of money on a set of scales.

3. Portrait of a Woman
Housed at the Archaeological Museum, this fresco depicts a women once believed to be the poet Sappho.

4. The Sacrifice of Iphigenia
Originally housed at the House of the Tragic Poet, this shows a naked Iphigenia taken to be sacrificed.

5. Cupids
In the dining room of the House of the Vettii is a colourful fresco depicting a series of cupids.

6. Ancient Pizza
This small fresco, not yet on public display, depicts a pizza prototype.

7. Sale of Bread
This fresco depicts a politician passing bread to voters.

8. Colosseum Riot
Found in the House of Actius Anicetus, this fresco depicts a riot that broke out in 59 CE.

9. The Black Room
Unearthed in late 2024, the Black Room is a banqueting hall home to a fresco depicting the Prince of Troy.

10. Venus in the Shell
In the House of Venus is a painting of a naked Venus sailing in a shell.

Fresco in the House of Venus

PIAZZAS AND FOUNTAINS

1 Piazza del Plebiscito, Naples
Ⓐ M5

This vast urban space has been restored to its original grandeur. On one side is the church of San Francesco di Paola (p70) and on the other the Palazzo Reale (p22). The royal equestrian statues on the square are all by Canova.

2 Piazza Duomo, Ravello
Ⓐ E4

A visit to Ravello should begin in this charming piazza, as there are a number of different routes you can take from here. Staircases and ramped walkways lead off in all directions.

3 Piazza San Domenico Maggiore
Ⓐ N2

Named after the massive church that towers above the square, this piazza is flanked on three sides by historic palaces and adorned with an obelisk.

Patrons seated on the Piazza San Domenico Maggiore

4 Piazza Bellini, Naples
Ⓐ N2

This is one of central Naples' most charming squares. With inviting café tables lined up on the sunny side and elegant architecture facing all around, Piazza Bellini is a favourite local spot.

5 Piazza Dante, Naples
Ⓐ N2

Following Italian Unification, a statue of the poet Dante was placed in the centre of the broad curve of this square, which was accordingly renamed. Before that, the area was known as Largo del Mercatello, when it was a major marketplace. Today it is still a busy focal point of the old part of the city.

6 Fontana dell' Immacolatella, Naples
Ⓐ N6 **Ⓐ** Via Partenope, near Castel dell'Ovo

This Santa Lucia district landmark, composed of three triumphal arches, once adorned the Palazzo Reale. It

The ornate Fontana dell'Immacolatella

dates from 1601 and is by Pietro Bernini and Michelangelo Naccherino. This grand fountain stands at one end of the seafront Lungomare (p75), while the Sebeto Fountain, a later work by Cosimo Fanzago, marks the other end.

7 Fontana del Nettuno, Naples
⊠ M4

Shifted from its home on Via Medina in 2014, the beautiful Fountain of Neptune now graces a wide spot in Piazza del Municipio. The 17th-century masterpiece is the work of three artists, including Pietro Bernini.

8 La Piazzetta, Capri

Magnetic at any time, this is Capri's most popular spot (p111). Marked by a domed bell tower, it has many cafés with tables outside, surrounded by whitewashed arcades.

9 Piazza Tasso, Sorrento
⊠ D5

This piazza is the heart of Sorrento. Find a spot at a café surrounding the square to take it all in. Constructed over a deep ravine, the square is named after the 16th-century poet Torquato Tasso from Sorrento. From the piazza, a steep road leads down to Marina Piccola, where ferries arrive and depart.

10 Piazza Duomo, Amalfi
⊠ E5

Dominated by the steps up to the cathedral and the black-and-white design of the building and its bell tower, this square is a hub of café life.

TOP 10
PARKS AND GARDENS

1. Gardens of Augustus, Capri
The island's primary green spot, these picturesque gardens (p61) offer sweeping sea views.

2. Orto Botanico, Naples
The Royal Plant Garden (p85) was founded by Joseph Bonaparte in 1807.

3. Real Bosco di Capodimonte, Naples
⊠ K1
Established by Charles III, this royal park has numerous ancient trees.

4. Villa La Floridiana, Naples
These grounds (p60) have been a public park since the 1920s.

5. Villa Comunale, Naples
This large public park (p94) is famous for its statuary and fine structures.

6. Parco Virgiliano, Naples
This park's (p116) hilltop position provides fine panoramas.

7. Caserta Park, Naples
These 18th-century gardens (p116) were influenced by Versailles.

8. La Mortella, Ischia
⊠ A4 ⊡ F Calise 45, Forio
⊡ Apr–Oct: 9am–6pm Tue, Thu, Sat & Sun ⊠ lamortella.org ⊡
Ischia's fabulous gardens include rare species.

9. Santi Marcellino e Festo Cloister, Naples
⊠ P3 ⊡ Largo San Marcellino 10
⊡ 9am–7pm Mon–Fri
The site of former 8th-century monasteries enjoys fine views.

10. Villa Cimbrone, Ravello
Sitting high on a promontory, the villa (p60) has stunning views of the Mediterranean and the coastline.

Gardens of Augustus, Capri

MUSEUMS AND GALLERIES

1 Certosa e Museo di San Martino, Naples

This monastery complex *(p34)* is home to several collections of art. The Pinacoteca, comprising part of the Prior's Quarters, is notable for its works from the Renaissance and Baroque eras, many commissioned for the monastery. On the upper floors, 19th-century works convey the look and feel of Naples during Italian Unification. A section devoted to Nativity scenes demonstrates the power and beauty of this Neapolitan art form.

2 Museo di Capodimonte, Naples

This world-class museum *(p32)* also owes its main masterpieces to the Farnese Collection. Paintings run the gamut from medieval to contemporary.

3 Museo Archeologico Nazionale, Naples

An unsurpassable museum *(p28)* for Greco-Roman art, home to important pieces unearthed in Rome and in towns around Vesuvius. The experience is a total immersion in the life of the ancients – their religious beliefs, sports, eating habits and even their erotic misdemeanours.

4 Museobottega della Tarsialignea, Sorrento

🚇 D5 🏠 San Nicola 28 🕐 10am–5:30pm (Apr–Oct to 6pm) 🔗
This museum showcases a stunning collection of fine inlaid wooden furniture and other wooden decorative objects *(intarsio)*. The collection is housed in a beautiful restored palace.

Wooden desk, Museobottega della Tarsialignea

Series of Flemish tapestries,
Museo di Capodimonte

5 Pinacoteca Girolamini, Naples

🗺️ P2 🏛️ Duomo 142 🕐 Hours vary, chech website 🌐 bibliotecadeigirolamini. beniculturali.it 🛗

For Neapolitan Baroque lovers, this little-known gallery is a must. There are fine works by Caracciolo, Vaccaro, Giordano and Ribera.

6 Museo Nazionale della Ceramica Duca di Martina, Naples

Exquisite Italian pieces by Ginori and Capodimonte artisans are on display at this museum (p95) along with creations by the factories of Meissen, Limoges, Sèvres and Saint-Cloud. Majolica works from medieval times and an 8th-century ceramic collection from China and Japan are exhibited too. Highlights include Hispano-Moorish lustreware and 18th-century porcelain.

7 Museo Pignatelli, Naples

🗺️ K6 🏛️ Riviera di Chiaia 200 🕐 8:30am–5pm Wed–Mon 🛗

Built in 1826, the villa was donated to the state in 1952. The loveliest rooms are the red hall, furnished in Louis XVI style, the smoking room with leather-lined walls and the ballroom with its mirrors

and chandeliers. Also of particular interest is the Coach Museum. Today, the Villa Pignatelli often plays host to temporary exhibitions and concerts.

8 Museo della Carta, Amalfi

🗺️ E5 🏛️ Largo Fratelli Spacca 2 🕐 9:30am–1:30pm & 3–6pm Tue–Sun 🌐 museodellacarta.it 🛗

Set in a paper mill, this museum preserves one of Europe's oldest papermaking factories. In addition to the original stone vats and machinery, there's also an exhibit which traces the history of the paper industry.

9 Museo Archeologico di Pithecusae, Ischia

🗺️ A4 🏛️ Corso Angelo Rizzoli 210, Lacco Ameno 🕐 Hours vary, chech website 🌐 pithecusae.it 🛗

This museum, part of the 18th-century Villa Arbusto, features exhibits on the history of ancient Ischia. Among the most famous pots found at a nearby necropolis is a typical late geometric *krater* depicting a shipwreck scene.

10 Museo Archeologico, Paestum

The treasures (p47) here include ancient Greek tomb paintings that were discovered on the site in 1968. Others include bronze vases, terracotta votive figures and funerary furnishings.

ARTISTS AND THEIR MASTERPIECES

1 Pietro Cavallini
Many scholars now credit this Roman artist (c 1250–c 1330) with much of the St Francis fresco in Assisi, formerly attributed to Giotto. Cavallini's work in Naples includes *Scenes from the Lives of Christ and John the Baptist* in San Domenico Maggiore (*p86*).

2 Donatello
The bas-relief of the Assumption, the cardinal's head and the caryatid on the right of the Tomb of Cardinal Rinaldo Brancaccio in Sant'Angelo a Nilo church (*p86*) are assumed to be the only pieces that exist in Naples by this Florentine master (c 1386–1466).

3 Masaccio
A 15th-century *Crucifixion* by this Tuscan painter (1401–28) is one of the treasures on display at the Capodimonte Museum. The work is a blend of the formal medieval tradition and the vitality of the Renaissance. Of note are the anatomical accuracy of Christ's torso and the sense of drama created by the outstretched arms of Mary Magdalene.

4 Caravaggio
This Baroque master (1571–1610) created a lasting artistic revolution with his dramatic use of light and shade. He spent a year or so in Naples; among the works he completed here is *The Flagellation of Christ*, originally in San Domenico Maggiore but now in Capodimonte.

5 Titian
A consummate painter of the Venetian Renaissance, (c 1448–1576) Titian is represented in Naples by several works, all but one in the Capodimonte Museum. These include his sensuous masterpiece *Danaë* and the religious works *La Maddalena* and *L'Annunciazione*.

6 Sofonisba Anguissola
Anguissola (c 1532–1625) was a leading Renaissance portraitist and one of the few female court painters. Her sketch *Boy Bitten by a Crayfish*, now in Museo di Capodimonte (*p32*), impressed Michelangelo so much that he tutored her for two years.

7 Sandro Botticelli
Typical of this much-loved Florentine artist (1445–1510) is his *Madonna with Child and Two Angels* in the Capodimonte Museum. Although it is an early work, all of the hallmarks of the painter at his height are here: the delicacy of the veils, the refinement of features and the soulful eyes, evoking sublimity.

Madonna with Child and Two Angels by Sandro Botticelli

Triumph of Judith ceiling fresco
by Luca Giordano

8 Luca Giordano

One of the most prolific of Naples' Baroque artists (1634–1705), his paintings and frescoes are ubiquitous in the city, adorning churches and museums. Most significant is *Triumph of Judith* (1704) on the Treasury ceiling in the Certosa e Museo di San Martino *(p34)*.

9 Jusepe de Ribera

This Spanish painter (1591–1652), much influenced by Caravaggio, spent most of his life in Naples, where he created powerful works *(p36)*. These include his *San Sebastiano* in the Certosa e Museo di San Martino.

10 Artemisia Gentileschi

Artist Gentileschi (1593–1652) was known for her brutal, haunting and strong depictions of women from myths, allegories and the Bible, as well as her own struggle for justice after being sexually assaulted. Her astounding masterpiece *Judith Slaying Holofernes* is now in the Capodimonte.

TOP 10 WRITERS AND PHILOSPHERS

1. Virgil
The epic poet (70–19 BCE) lived in Naples for many years, incorporating local legends into his work *The Aeneid*.

2. Petronius
In his saga *The Satyricon* (only a fragment survives), this author (d 66 CE) captures the decadence of the Roman Empire in the villas of Naples.

3. Pliny the Younger
Thanks to this writer (c 62–113 CE) we know much about the day Vesuvius erupted *(p41)*.

4. Suetonius
The writer (70–126 CE) is famous for his *Twelve Caesars*, scandalous accounts of the first Roman emperors.

5. St Thomas Aquinas
The theologian (c 1225–74) was often a guest at San Domenico Maggiore, headquarters for religious study at the University of Naples.

6. Petrarch
The great lyric poet and scholar (1304–74) often visited the court of Robert of Anjou in Naples.

7. Giovanni Boccaccio
Author of *The Decameron* (1348–53), 10 tales of ribaldry in medieval Naples.

8. Torquato Tasso
Tasso (1544–95) was an epic poet and a native of Sorrento.

9. Giambattista Vico
Born in Naples, Vico (1668–1744) found fame with his influential *La Scienza Nuova (The New Science)* published in 1725.

10. Benedetto Croce
The philosopher, historian and statesman (1866–1952) spent most of his life in Naples.

Statue of writer Giovanni Boccaccio

Posing with the famous Pulcinella bronze statue

ON STAGE, PAGE AND SCREEN

1 Pulcinella
Cunning, perpetually hungry and rambunctious, Pulcinella ("little chick") is the symbol of Neapolitans and their streetwise way of life. Ubiquitous in Neapolitan theatre through the ages, his signature white pyjama-like outfit, peaked hat and hook-nosed mask go back to ancient Roman burlesque, in which a bawdy clown, Maccus, was one of the stock characters.

2 Opera in Naples
Naples played a seminal role in popularizing opera in the late 17th and early 18th centuries, with Neapolitan composers such as Leonardo Vinci and Leonardo Leo writing versatile operas to be staged at the San Carlo (p94).

3 Scugnizzi and Lazzaroni
These two characters, products of the poverty the city has historically suffered, are street urchins and ruffians. They have been the inspiration for numerous plays and books, with variations on these stock characters a common trope in Neapolitan literature.

4 Neapolitan Song
Naples has always been known as a city of music, with plaintive songs focusing nostalgically on love, the sun and the sea. "'O sole mio" and "Santa Lucia" are the most renowned.

5 Totò
This rubber-faced comedian was the quintessence of Italian humour. Until his death in 1967, "The Prince of Laughter" made five films a year, some of them comic masterpieces, including Miseria e nobiltà (Poverty and Nobility, 1954) and La banda degli onesti (The Band of Honest Men, 1956).

6 Pino Daniele
Known as the voice of Naples, Pino Daniele was one of Italy's most popular singer-songwriters. He was known for his songs "Quando" and "Je so' pazzo". After his death in 2015, a street in Naples was named in his honour.

7 Massimo Troisi
Embodying the heart of the Neapolitan character, this actor made international waves with Il Postino (The Postman), nominated for an

Academy Award in 1995. Sadly, just hours after the film was completed, Troisi died at the age of 41.

8 The Elena Ferrante Effect

Elena Ferrante's *L'amica geniale* (*My Brilliant Friend*) became a literary sensation when it was published in 2011. Three more novels in the series followed, all set in and around Naples. Many sites from the book – and the HBO TV series, *My Brilliant Friend* (2018) – can be visited today.

9 Naples on Screen

Naples and the Amalfi Coast have provided the setting for numerous films over the years. Notable ones include Roberto Rossellini's *Viaggio in Italia* (*Journey to Italy, 1954*) and Francesco Rosi's *Le mani sulla città* (*Hands over the City, 1963*). More recently, the Netflix series *Ripley* (2024) was shot in Naples and Atrani.

10 Sophia Loren

One of the most talented and iconic Italian actresses, Sophia Loren was best-known for her performance in the 1954 film *L'oro di Napoli* (*The Gold of Naples*). Popularly known as "La Loren", she went on to build a successful and formidable career as a Hollywood star.

Sophia Loren in *L'oro di Napoli* (*The Gold of Naples*)

TOP 10
OPERA LEGENDS

Portrait of Gaetano Donizetti

1. Gaetano Donizetti
Donizetti composed 16 operas for the San Carlo.

2. Castrati
An 18th-century Neapolitan speciality, renowned *castrati* included Farinelli (Carlo Broschi) and Giovanni Battista Velluti.

3. Giovanni Battista Pergolesi
Most of this Baroque composer's operas premiered in Naples.

4. Giovanni Paisiello
This composer's operatic style had a strong influence on Mozart and Rossini.

5. Domenico Cimarosa
A composer of the Neapolitan School, Cimarosa wrote more than 80 operas including *Il matrimonio segreto* (*The Secret Marriage, 1792*).

6. Wolfgang Amadeus Mozart
Mozart's father, Leopold, took him to Naples in 1770 when he was 13 years old to educate him in opera.

7. Gioachino Rossini
The composer was artistic director of Teatro San Carlo between 1815 and 1822.

8. Vincenzo Bellini
In 1826 Bellini staged his first work at the San Carlo, *Bianca e Gernando*.

9. Giuseppe Verdi
The "god" of Italian opera wrote his first opera for the theatre, *Alzira*, in 1845.

10. Enrico Caruso
Arguably the most famous tenor ever, Caruso was born in Naples in 1873.

INSPIRING SPOTS

1 Monastero Santa Rosa, Conca dei Marini
▣ E5 ▣ Via Roma 2 ☏ 089 832 11 99
This former monastery *(p132)* is the dream hotel for an inspiring escape on the Amalfi Coast. Wander through the terraced gardens or enjoy a dip in the beautiful infinity pool.

2 Villa La Floridiana, Naples
▣ J4 ▣ Via Domenico Cimarosa 77 ▣ 9:30am–5pm Wed–Mon
Lucia Migliaccio, Duchess of Floridia, once called this sumptuous place home. It was a love token from her husband, Ferdinand I, whose morganatic wife she became soon after the death of his first wife, Maria Carolina of Austria. Not only is the story romantic but the situation itself affords some of the finest views of the city and the bay. The gardens are an excellent place for a peaceful stroll, and the main building now houses a museum filled with a number of delightful treasures.

3 Le Sirenuse, Positano
In the heart of Positano, Le Sirenuse *(p132)* has earned its reputation as one of the most beautiful hotels on the Amalfi Coast. Even if you're not a guest, you can enjoy an unforgettable meal with a view at the elegant La Sponda restaurant.

4 Ristorante Da Adolfo, Positano
▣ E5 ▣ Via Laurito 40
Ⓦ daadolfo.com
Hidden away in a tiny cove just east of Positano is the tranquil Laurito beach. Since 1966, the beach's restaurant has been serving freshly caught fish, mozzarella grilled on lemon leaves, and locally made wine with fresh peaches. The restaurant offers a free boat service for clients from Positano's main pier and the ride is five minutes long. Sunbeds and umbrellas are available to rent, so arrive early for a romantic day at the beach.

5 Villa Cimbrone, Ravello
▣ E5 ▣ Via Santa Chiara 26
▣ 9am–6:30pm daily Ⓦ hotelvilla-cimbrone.com 🡕
Declared by American writer Gore Vidal to be one of the most beautiful places

Quiet spot in the remarkable Villa Cimbrone

on earth, this clifftop, 12th-century villa is famous for its terraced, maze-like gardens. The highlight is the Terrace of Infinity, which offers breathtaking views over the dramatic coastline and the Mediterranean.

6 Marechiaro

This fishing village *(p115)* between the tip of Capo di Posillipo and Punta del Cavallo is famous with locals for its romantic atmosphere. The vista from here is said to be so gorgeous that even the fish come here to woo their sweethearts by the moonlight. There are many excellent restaurants around the prime viewing spot, all specializing in fish.

7 Le Grottelle Restaurant, Capri

U1 🏛 Via Arco Naturale 13 📞 081 837 57 19 🕒 Tue (except Jul & Aug)

The cuisine here is simple, homemade fare that includes seafood, pasta, chicken and perhaps rabbit, while the wine is local and very creditable. What makes it so romantic is the setting. Not only is it close to nature, situated near the Arco Naturale,

Enjoying the breathtaking view from Le Grottelle Restaurant

but the terrace tables also enjoy an eye-popping view straight down to the sea, along a precipitous ravine. In addition, the friendly owners do their best to make any meal a memorable event.

8 Villa Eva Resort, Anacapri

Set amid subtropical gardens, this resort consists of a main house and bungalows. Each accommodation is unique and there's a wonderful grand piano-shaped pool.

9 Gardens of Augustus, Capri

U2 🏛 Viale Matteotti 14/16
🕒 9:30am–8pm daily

The marvellous views from the Gardens of Augustus make Capri one of the most romantic spots. The gardens are perfect for admiring the Faraglioni rocks, zigzagging Via Krupp and the mesmerizing turquoise sea.

10 Villa Maria Restaurant, Ravello

This stunning restaurant serves superb food. Sit at a table in its vine-covered garden for gorgeous views over the scenic coastline and sparkling sea below. Part of the Hotel Villa Maria *(p131)*, it is one of Ravello's best restaurants, specializing in fresh fish and various seafood dishes as well as local wines. The delectable lemon mousse is a must-try.

BEACHES

1 Marina di Praia
⌖ E5

This small cove, just beyond Positano (*p44*), has a bit of beach. However you will share the cove with local fishing boats, a couple of bar-restaurants, a diving centre and the coast's premier disco, Africana.

2 Posillipo and Beyond
⌖ J2

The nearest beaches to the centre of Naples can be found at Posillipo, although most are shingle, not sand, and the water isn't quite clean. At the ends of the Cumana and Circumflegrea railways, there are more sandy beaches, albeit not entirely pristine.

3 Sorrento

Sorrento (*p107*) has bathing platforms, with lifts or steps leading down to them from several hotels. This is a paid facility unless you are a hotel guest. Elsewhere there's a fine beach to the east, at Meta di Sorrento, while westwards, there's a small sandy beach at Marina di Puolo and another at Marina di Lobra.

4 Capri

There are few sandy beaches here, although small ones can be found around Marina Grande (*p42*). A popular pebbly choice is Marina Piccola. Head down to the bottom of Via Krupp, where huge flat stones lie along the shore.

5 Marina di Furore
⌖ E5

A very precipitous path goes straight down to this dramatic, tiny beach set between the cliffs. A few fishers's homes cluster here, with their boats neatly moored along one side, and there's a bar-restaurant.

6 Amalfi

Lined with colourful umbrellas, the Marina Grande beach at Amalfi has a free area popular with locals. You can

Sunseekers at the Marina di Furore beach

Lovely beach and harbour of the Marina di Praia

take a short boat ride to the rocky Santa Croce beach.

7 Positano
At the beach resorts of this town *(p45)*, payment is necessary for a sunbed and an umbrella. Or take the path to the west, around the cliff, to the beach at Fornillo – it's smaller and rockier but more relaxed.

8 Procida
This small island *(p106)* has several good beaches. One of the longest stretches from Chiaiolella Marina to Ciraccio, called the Lido, is the island's most popular beach so expect crowds. From here a bridge leads to the nature reserve of Vivara, which has rocky access to the sea. To the northeast, Pozzo Vecchio also has a beach.

9 Ischia
For a small fee, you can use two sunbeds and an umbrella at any beach here *(p104)*. There are plenty to choose from, including sandy stretches in Forio and Ischia Porto.

10 Erchie and Cetara
🔲 F4–F5
The beach at Erchie is a small cove with a watchtower and fishing boats. At Cetara, bathers share the narrow rocky strip with boats, but it's good for a dip.

TOP 10
SPAS

1. Terme di Agnano, Naples
🔲 J2 🏠 Via Agnano Astroni 24
This spa has been running since ancient times. It is known for its mud-baths and mineral waters.

2. Giardini Poseidon Terme, Ischia
🔲 B4 🏠 Via Giovanni Mazzella
Saunas, Jacuzzis, pools and treatments – all are available here.

3. Negombo, Ischia
🔲 A4 🏠 Via San Montano, Lacco Ameno
Negombo is surrounded by beautiful gardens with volcanic springs.

4. Terme Capasso, Contursi
🏠 Via Nazionale Bagni
There's a large outdoor thermal park and spa here.

5. Terme Belliazzi, Ischia
🔲 A4 🏠 Piazza Bagni del Gurgitello 122, Casamicciola
Mud treatments and massages are among the many rejuvenating options here.

6. Terme di Cavascura, Ischia
🔲 A4 🏠 Via Cavascura, Serrara Fontana
Built into the cliffs, the Terme di Cavascura has a cave sauna and baths in sulphurous water.

7. Terme della Regina Isabella, Ischia
🔲 A4 🏠 Piazza Santa Restituta 1, Lacco Ameno
Luxury massages, treatments, a wide range of therapies and diet and fitness programmes are on offer here.

8. Capri Palace Hotel
Anacapri's top hotel *(p133)* also has a spa and beauty treatment centre.

9. Hotel Capo La Gala, Vico Equense
🔲 D4 🏠 Via Luigi Serio 8
Take a dip in the mineral water swimming pool at this hotel.

10. Parco Termale Aphrodite Apollon, Ischia
🔲 A4 🏠 Via Petrelle, Sant'Angelo
Pools, saunas and massages are available at this spa.

Via dei Tribunali, the city's ancient thoroughfare

WALKS

1 Decumano Maggiore
🅿 P2

The ancient "decumanus maggiore" was the main east-west artery of Naples, now known as Via dei Tribunali. Decumano Maggiore constitutes the heart of the old quarter and is replete with unmissable sights, as well as intriguing shops and bars and cafés to while away the hours.

2 Royal Naples
🅿 N4

For regal edifices and elegant cafés and shops, this choice part of town is pedestrian-friendly. A good place to start is the Fontana del Nettuno (p53) in Piazza Municipio and then head towards the sea and west. This arc takes in Castel Nuovo, Teatro di San Carlo and Galleria Umberto I.

3 Capri

Once you break away from the smart shops and hotels, this island (p42) is all about nature walks: up to Villa Jovis, down to the Arco Naturale, along the Sentiero dei Fortini to the Blue Grotto – the possibilities are numerous.

4 Spaccanapoli

The colloquial name of this ancient street (p82) means "Splits Naples", which is exactly what it does, cutting the oldest part of the city right down the middle. Beginning at the western end in Piazza del Gesù Nuovo, a straight line takes you past some of the city's finest monuments, and there are shops, bars, cafés and pizzerias.

5 Lungomare
🅿 N6

Beginning at the public gardens next to the Palazzo Reale, take the seaside road around the Santa Lucia quarter and past some of Naples' loveliest areas, including the island of Castel dell'Ovo and the green splendour of the Villa Comunale.

6 Via Toledo
🅿 N3

Via Toledo starts in the royal quarter before running past the Quartieri Spagnoli (Spanish District) – a warren of narrow, dark streets that hide some of the city's best-kept secrets. Continuing on, you'll pass Piazza Dante and finally reach the Museo Archeologico (p28).

7 Sorrentine Peninsula
🅿 D5

If you take the *funivia* (cable car) from Castellammare di Stabia up to Monte

Faito there are startling views from the top, as well as the beginning of many nature trails, some of which eventually lead as far as Positano.

8 The Amalfi Coast

Hiking points can be reached above Positano and between Ravello and Amalfi and Atrani. Most of these paths are erstwhile goat trails – the most famous is the Sentiero degli Dei (Path of the Gods) – while some have been built up as stone stairways; all offer incomparable views.

9 Ischia

The island of Ischia (p104) has several hiking trails catering to various fitness levels and interests. A memorable trek is up Monte Epomeo from Forio, passing through the picturesque village of Fontana. It takes about 40 minutes to complete the hike.

10 Vesuvius

A walk along the rim of this vast crater (p100) is an experience of a lifetime. Some 20,000 visitors a year trek to the top to peer into the steaming depths 200 m (700 ft) below. The steep hike up takes about 30 minutes and it's at its best in late spring, when flowers are most vibrant.

Hiking the trail around the rim of Mount Vesuvius

TOP 10 DRIVES

Scenic Amalfi Coast road

1. Positano to Vietri
◉ E5
Single road "of 1,000 turns".

2. Sorrento to Positano
◉ D5
Follow the signs to Santa Agata sui Due Golfi and then Colli di Fontanelle to get your first glimpse of Positano.

3. Amalfi to Ravello
◉ E5
Leave the coast road and climb up for a vista unlike any other.

4. Over the Monti Lattari
◉ E5
Wind through mountain meadows before the descent to the Amalfi Coast.

5. Around Ischia
◉ B4
A fairly good road rings the island.

6. Naples to Sorrento
◉ E4
Cut off the tollway to Castellammare di Stabia and take the picturesque road.

7. Marina Grande to Anacapri, Capri
◉ S1
Enjoy the ride in a classic open-top taxi.

8. The Phlegraean Fields
◉ J2
Drive coastal to Pozzuoli, then inland to Terme di Agnano and La Solfatara.

9. Cumae
◉ B3
Begin at Lago d'Averno and pass under the Arco Felice to arrive at Cumae.

10. Naples to Paestum
◉ H6
Take the A3, then switch to the S19, direction Battipaglia. Take the right fork for Paestum, on the S18 south.

OFF THE BEATEN TRACK

1 San Gennaro Catacombs

K1 **Via Capodimonte 13**
catacombedinapoli.it

Burials here date from the 2nd century. In the 5th century, the body of San Gennaro, Naples' patron saint, was brought here, and the place became a pilgrimage site. Frescoes and mosaics on the two levels of this vast layout attest to its importance.

2 Napoli Sotterranea

P2 **Piazza S Gaetano 69**
napolisotterranea.org

This tour's entrance is next to San Paolo Maggiore (p86) and takes you into a world of excavations that date back to the 4th century BCE. It is advisable to bring a jacket as it can be cool. The digging began when the Greeks quarried large tufa blocks to build the city of Neapolis. Caves were also dug here to be used as tombs. Centuries later the Romans transformed this underground area into aqueducts and cisterns, which were in use until the cholera epidemic of 1884.

3 San Gaudioso Catacombs

K1 **Basilica of Santa Maria della Sanità, Via della Sanità 124**
catacombedinapoli.it

Originally built by the Romans for use as cisterns, this labyrinth of underground tunnels evolved into catacombs in the 5th century, when St Gaudiosus, a North African bishop and hermit, was interred here. The remains of fresco and mosaic decorations can still be seen.

4 Spiaggia di Fornillo, Positano

This is an alternative to the main beach at Positano. To get to Fornillo, head west on the path past the Lo Guarracino restaurant, around the cliff. It's a rocky beach, overlooked by two towers, but there's a café-restaurant and other facilities that you can explore.

5 Cimitero delle Fontanelle

K1 **Via delle Fontanelle 80**
338 965 22 88 **10am–5pm daily**

Once a Roman quarry for tufa blocks, this cavern became a depository for the city's dead during the cholera epidemic of 1884. Graves and tombs were emptied all over Naples and the skulls stacked here – some 40,000 in all, with the addition of many more during the cholera outbreak of 1973.

Frescoes in the tunnel of the San Gaudioso Catacombs

6 Parco Sommerso, Baia

🗺 B3

Most of the ancient city of Baia (p51) now lies underwater. Just below the surface of the water are remnants of the port and parts of various villas and temples.

7 Sibyl's Grotto, Cumae

This grotto is believed to be a Roman military structure by some and a mythological one by others. The wedge-shaped walls, coupled with the lighting, create a hypnotic effect.

8 Tomb of Virgil and Crypta Neapolitana

🗺 K2 📍 Salita della Grotta 20, Mergellina 🕐 8:45am–2:15pm Wed–Mon

What is known as Virgil's tomb is a Roman burial vault from the Augustan age. It is a typical dovecote style of burial, with niches for urns containing the ashes of the deceased. Next to the tomb are a tufa quarry and a *crypta* (tunnel) from the 1st century BCE.

9 MADRE

🗺 P1 📍 Via Settembrini 79 🕐 10am–7:30pm Wed–Mon, 10am–8pm Sun 🌐 madrenapoli.it ♿

This museum of contemporary art is housed in a 14th-century church. Exhibitions from the 1940s onwards contrast with the surrounding history of Naples. Permanent exhibitions include the Historical Collection. Book your visit in advance online.

10 Green Grotto, Capri

🗺 T2

On the other side of the island from its more famous sibling, the Blue Grotto (p43), this smaller cave glows emerald-green once you duck inside. The best way to get here is to join a boat tour of the whole island from Marina Grande or rent a kayak at Punta Carena. The grotto can be closed during high tides or rough seas.

Tour boats at the Green Grotto in Capri

FAMILY ATTRACTIONS

Swimming in the calm waters, Marina Piccola beach

1 Marina Piccola Beach, Capri

One of the most child-friendly beaches in the area, Capri has tranquil waters and well-protected bathing areas. There are handy toy and swimming gear shops, and a choice of places to eat. Changing rooms and sunbeds are available.

2 Villa Comunale

This urban park (p94) in central Naples has a playground for kids and plenty of gardens and walk-ways for families to enjoy. The biggest attraction here is the Stazione Zoologica (Zoological Institute), one of the oldest aquariums in Europe.

3 Edenlandia

J2 J F Kennedy 76, Fuorigrotta 4–10pm Mon–Fri, 10:30am–1:30pm Sat & Sun edenlandia.it

Established in 1965, this ageing amusement park is a favourite among the locals. Rides include a Big Dipper, a Ghost Train, a Canoe Flume and Bumper Cars, as well as several more hightech options. An old-fashioned choice that never fails to delight is the Little Train, which covers about 0.5 km (0.30 mile) as it transports visitors through the park.

4 Vesuvius

No child will ever forget a trip up this volcano (p100) and a peek over the rim into the steaming abyss below. It's a fairly short, steep walk – only about half an hour – and the thrill will stay with them for years.

5 Pietrarsa Railway Museum

L2 Pietrarsa 9:30am–8pm Thu, 9:30am–7:30pm Fri, 9:30am–7:30pm Sat, Sun & hols museopietrarsa.it

Italy's first railway was inaugurated by King Ferdinand II in 1839 and 150 years later the railway workshop was opened as a museum. It is the largest of its kind in Europe and has impressive displays,

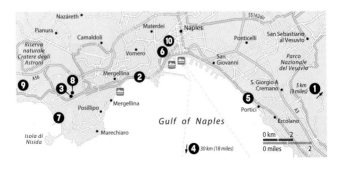

Vintage steam locomotives, Pietrarsa Railway Museum

such as a reconstruction of the first royal train and a line-up of the later, lavishly gilded carriages. On Wednesdays it is open by prior reservation only.

6 Centro Musei delle Scienze Naturali

📍P3 🏠 Via Mezzocannone 8 & Largo S Marcellino 10 🕐 Mon–Wed & Fri; hours vary check website 🌐 cmsnf.it ♿

The Università di Napoli Federico II houses five museums in one building with sections on Physics, Mineralogy (currently closed for renovation), Anthropology, Zoology and Palaeontology, the latter with fascinating dinosaur exhibits.

7 Science City

A hands-on "experimentorium" (p118), with something to offer for all age groups. The exhibits at the Science City include amazing up-to-date computer gizmos that seem to transcend language barriers and a planetarium.

8 Zoo di Napoli

📍J2 🏠 Via J F Kennedy 76 📞081 193 631 54 🕐 9:30am–6pm Mon–Fri, 9:30am–7pm Sat, Sun & hols ♿

This zoo is home to more than 400 animals, including monkeys, lions, kangaroos and zebras. A variety of engaging educational activities are also organized for kids.

9 Teatro dei Piccoli

📍J2 🏠 Via Antoniotto Usodimare 200 🕐 9am–5pm Mon–Fri 🌐 teatrodeipiccoli.it ♿

Teatro dei Piccoli hosts magic shows, puppet shows, and musical and theatrical performances. It also arranges wonderful workshops and activities for children. Book tickets online in advance for performances.

10 Ospedale delle Bambole

📍P2 🏠 Via S Biagio dei Librai 39 🕐 10:30am–1:30pm & 2:30–5:30pm Fri–Sun 🌐 ospedale dellebambole.com

Children are captivated by the unique concept of the Doll Hospital and attracted by the array of dolls that are here waiting to be "cured". This fascinating workshop also repairs wooden dolls and toy accessories. There's a shop selling dolls, so your child won't necessarily have to say goodbye to a new-found friend.

Puppets on display in the Ospedale delle Bambole

CHURCHES IN NAPLES

1 San Francesco di Paola

A rarity in Naples, this Neo-Classical structure (p93) was inspired by the Pantheon, Rome's great pagan temple to the gods built in the 2nd century CE. Inside and out, the basilica is austere, with the exception of the poly-chrome marble Baroque altar that has many statues.

2 Duomo

The oldest wing of Naples' cathedral (p26) is the city's most ancient surviving building, a Paleo-Christian church dating back to the 4th century. The cathedral also has the oldest baptistry in the western world, with glorious mosaics. Archaeological excavations here have revealed structures reaching as far back as the ancient Greeks.

3 Santa Chiara

The original church (p83) here was built in 1310 and, after various renovations, it has been returned to its glorious Gothic style. The most

Colourful pillars and majolica tiles, Santa Chiara

famous feature is the adjoining convent's beautiful 18th-century majolica cloister.

4 Basilica dell'Incoronata Madre del Buon Consiglio

Q K1 **A** Via Capodimonte 13
W basilicacapodimonte.it

The ornate basilica of Madre del Buon Consiglio (Crowned Mother of Good Counsel) was built in the 20th century but appears to be older, given its similarity to St Peter's in Rome. It houses works of art from various closed, damaged or abandoned places of worship throughout the city.

5 Santa Maria Maggiore

Q N2 **A** Piazzetta Pietrasanta 17/18 **O** 10am–7pm daily
W polopietrasanta.it

Nicknamed *Pietrasanta* (holy stone) after its ancient stone marked with a cross, thought to grant indulgences to whoever kissed it, the original church here was built in the 10th and 11th centuries and the bell tower is Naples' only example of early medieval architecture. The present church, however, is Baroque.

9 Santa Lucia
🚇 N6 🏠 Via Santa Lucia 3
🕐 8am–1pm & 5–8pm Mon–Sat,
8:30am–1:30pm & 5:30–8pm Sun &
hols 🌐 santaluciaamare.it

According to legend a church stood
here in ancient times, but as per
experts, the earliest structure can
be traced back to the 9th century.
Destroyed and rebuilt many times,
the present church is a postwar
structure. The artworks were
destroyed during World War II,
save an 18th-century statue of
St Lucy and two paintings.

6 San Lorenzo Maggiore
One of Naples' oldest monuments,
this church (p86) is a mix of Gothic and
Baroque styles. The cloister has access
to Greco-Roman remains, including
part of a Roman market.

7 Pio Monte della Misericordia
🚇 Q2 🏠 Via dei Tribunali 253
🕐 10am–6pm Mon–Sat, 9am–
2:30pm Sun 🌐 piomontedella
misericordia.it

This institution was founded in
1601, inspired by Counter-Reformation
precepts which gave weight to such
works as a way of ensuring salvation.
The church is set back from the street
by a loggia, where pilgrims could find
shelter. The altarpiece, *The Seven Acts
of Mercy* by Caravaggio, is an allegory
of charitable deeds. Upstairs is an
art collection.

8 Certosa e Museo di San Martino
The location of this sparkling white
monastery complex (p34) attests to
the erstwhile wealth and power of its
monks. In the 17th and 18th centuries
they commissioned the greatest artists
of the day to embellish their church
and chambers in Baroque style – the
church, in particular, is a flamboyant
catalogue of colour and pattern,
sporting at least one work by each
and every famous hand of the age.

10 Santa Maria del Parto
🚇 J2 🏠 Via Mergellina
🕐 8:30am–7pm daily
🌐 santamariadelparto.it

Renaissance poet and humanist
Jacopo Sannazaro ordered this
church to be built in the 16th century
and his tomb behind the high altar
is notable for its lack of Christian
symbolism. In a side chapel the
painting of the Archangel Michael
searing the "Mergellina Devil" depicts
a bishop's spiritual victory in over-
coming temptation when a woman
tried to enchant him with a spell.

NEAPOLITAN DISHES

A plate of spaghetti served with lobster

1 Primo
This course usually means pasta or rice, but *minestre* and *zuppe* (soups) also appear in this category. Great *primi* to look out for are *spaghetti alle vongole veraci* (with clams), *pasta e fagioli* (with beans), *fettuccine alla puttanesca* (egg noodles with tomato, capers, black olives and red pepper) and *risotto alla pescatora* (rice with seafood).

2 Dolci
Many Neapolitan desserts are inspired by their Sicilian cousins, notably *delizie*, a cream-filled cake, and *panna cotta* (cooked cream), perhaps topped with fresh fruit. In season, the melon, figs and wild strawberries are unforgettable.

3 Contorni
The fertility of the land around Naples is most evident when you taste the produce it brings forth. For *contorni* (side dishes), peppers, artichokes, aubergine (eggplant), capers, mushrooms and green beans are offered steamed or sautéed. Expect the freshness to have been retained fully, cooked with a touch of garlic, tomato or lemon, and herbs.

4 Secondo
Main course dishes come in two varieties, *mare* (sea) and *terra* (land). Fresh seafood, especially *vongole* (clams) and *cozze* (mussels), are popular along the coast. Meat dishes are varied and include *polpette* (meatballs), *salsiccia* (sausage) with broccoli and *coniglio* (rabbit), a speciality on Ischia.

5 Fish and Seafood
This category is the area's strong point. *Calamari* (squid) are a favourite, as are *cozze* (mussels) in a variety of presentations. *Seppie* (cuttlefish) and *polipo* (octopus) are popular, too, stewed, fried or steamed. *Pesce all'acqua pazza* (fish in "crazy water") is a treat – fresh fish stewed in water with tomatoes, garlic and chillies.

6 Insalata
Besides the host of fresh leaves and cherry tomatoes that end up in the wonderful salads (*insalata*) here, there are two famous cold dishes from the area. The *insalata caprese* is the essence of simplicity, relying on quality *mozzarella di bufala*, tomatoes and aromatic basil. *Caponata* may include marinated aubergine (eggplant), artichoke hearts and capers, with bread to soak up the flavours.

A bowl of fresh caprese salad

Pastries for sale on display in a café in Naples

7 Pastries

A *sfogliatella* (pastry filled with ricotta cheese) is a sublime way to start the day, accompanied by a cup of coffee. Other treats include *babà* (cake soaked in rum and honey) and *zeppole* (pastry filled with custard and topped with wild cherries).

8 Formaggi

Mozzarella di bufala is the signature cheese from the area. The milk of the buffalo has a tangy quality and the cheese a unique smoothness. The smoked version is *provola*.

9 Antipasti

The first course may be seafood or marinated fish, a selection of olives and cured meats, *bruschetta* (toasted bread) with various toppings or *prosciutto* (ham), all served with fresh figs or sweet melon, depending on the season.

10 Pizza

Fresh San Marzano tomatoes and top-quality flour mean Neapolitan pizza is inimitable. It's spongy, chewy, succulent and melts in your mouth, while the toppings are flavourful and aromatic. Purists insist that it was invented here centuries ago and that the only true pizza is the margherita – tomato, basil and mozzarella cheese, with olive oil.

TOP 10
LOCAL DRINKS

1. White Wine
Campania wines are of a very high quality. Falanghina, Greco di Tufo and Lacryma Christi are reliable names.

2. Red Wine
Full-bodied reds come from the local Aglianico grape.

3. Spremute
Most bars are set up, in summer, to turn out freshly squeezed orange juice and a local version of lemonade.

4. Beer
All major brands are available, but a local Italian favourite is Peroni. If you want draught, ask for *alla spina*.

5. Mineral Water
Italians enjoy a huge array of mineral waters. A great choice is Ferrarelle – or for something lighter, Uliveto.

6. Digestivi
Many restaurants produce their own digestive concoctions – pure alcohol with a soothing mixture of spices and flavourings.

7. Coffee
Neapolitan-style coffee traditionally comes already sweetened, and it is generally very concentrated.

8. Soft Drinks
An interesting Italian cola-type drink other than the usuals is Chinotto.

9. Infusioni
Camomilla (camomile) is considered to be a relaxant, while other herbal teas on offer include *menta* (peppermint) and *tiglio* (lime-tree).

10 Liqueurs
The most famous is the lemon liqueur *limoncello*, which delivers quite a kick.

***Limoncello* alcoholic drink**

NAPLES AND THE AMALFI COAST FOR FREE

Towering glass skylights of Galleria Umberto I

1 Galleria Umberto I, Naples

The Neo-Renaissance designs, soaring glass roof and marble floors of the Galleria Umberto I *(p94)* make this 19th-century shopping gallery worth seeing for its architecture alone.

2 Arco Naturale, Capri

While the price tag of many of Capri's sights can shock, the natural beauty is as easy on the eyes as it is on the budget. For a beautiful walk, follow signs from the Piazzetta in Capri Town to the Arco Naturale.

3 Villa Romana, Minori

For a glimpse of ancient Roman history, visit the ruins of this wealthy family villa *(p109)* that have been excavated in the heart of Minori.

4 Spaccanapoli, Naples

This narrow main street cuts straight through the historic centre *(p82)* of the city and captures the vibrant atmosphere that is Naples. Enjoy a stroll past fine monuments while visiting free churches like the Gesù Nuovo and San Domenico Maggiore *(p86)*. Today, the street is officially named Via Benedetto Croce and moving east it changes to Via San Biagio dei Librai.

5 Via Positanesi d'America, Positano

Connecting Positano's Spiaggia Grande with the more secluded Spiaggia di Fornillo *(p66)*, this cliff-hugging

pathway is one of the prettiest walks on the Amalfi Coast, with beautiful views over Positano.

6 Marina Grande, Sorrento
D5

Sorrento's Marina Grande harbour is one of the most charming spots in town, with its rows of colourful fishing boats bobbing in the water and multihued homes that were once home to fishers.

7 Auditorium Oscar Niemeyer, Ravello
E4 **Via della Repubblica 12**
089 85 83 60

This rare example of modern design is named after its creator, Brazilian architect Oscar Niemeyer. While only open for events, its large terrace offers the same outstanding views you would pay to see at the Villa Rufolo nearby.

8 Lungomare Caracciolo, Naples

Stretching along the Bay of Naples, Lungomare is a pedestrianized waterfront promenade with panoramic views of the city and Castel dell'Ovo (p94). It is the perfect place for an evening *passeggiata*.

9 Duomo, Naples

While there is an admission charge to visit the cathedral's museum and archaeological area, it is free to visit the soaring nave of the Duomo (p26) and the dazzling Cappella di San Gennaro.

10 Villa Comunale, Naples

This 18th-century urban park (p94) was designed by Luigi Vanvitelli, the mastermind behind the grandiose Reggia di Caserta. With playgrounds, classic statues and beautiful views, it's a family friendly spot to while away an afternoon.

Arco Naturale overlooking the sea in Capri

TOP 10 BUDGET TIPS

Street food on offer

1. Naples is famous for its street food, which is a delicious way to save money and experience local specialities.

2. Visit Naples from October to April (but not Christmas) when low-season rates and discounts will delight the budget-minded traveller.

3. Note that many hotels and restaurants on the Amalfi Coast and Capri close during the winter, however, rates are often lower for the shoulder season October to November and February to March.

4. Most beaches have a *spiaggia libera* area where you do not have to pay to access the beach.

5. Parking can be exceedingly expensive and limited on the Amalfi Coast, so traveling by public transport is recommended.

6. Save money on visits to many sights in Naples and throughout the region with the Campania Artecard, see campaniartecard.it.

7. Take the Circumvesuviana train for an inexpensive way to travel between Naples, Sorrento, Pompeii and Herculaneum.

8. The ferry between Positano and Amalfi is an affordable way to see the beauty of the Amalfi Coast from the sea.

9. Alibus runs a cheap shuttle from the Naples airport to the Napoli Centrale train station and port.

10. Many archaeological sites and museums offer a free open day during the week or month.

FESTIVALS AND EVENTS

1 Movie Magic
Naples and its surrounds play host to a number of big-screen events. In early January, the region's most glamorous island presents the glitzy Capri, Hollywood International Film Festival *(capri-world.com)*, while the week-long Napoli Film Festival *(napolifilmfestival. com)* in September showcases work by lesser-known filmmakers.

2 Pyrotechnic Performances
The region loves to mark festivities with eye-popping firework displays. Huge fireworks shimmer over Naples in February to honour Saint Biagio, and the pyrotechnics that light up Positano in August at Ferragosto (the feast of the Assumption) are absolutely stunning.

3 Carnevale
Held just before Lent, this age-old celebration sees the area indulge in delicious food and lively pageantry. Pulcinella *(p58)* – a Neapolitan comic character – is lord of this blow-out in Naples. On the Amalfi Coast, the town of Maiori hosts a parade of colourful floats.

4 Easter
In Italy, Pasqua (Easter Sunday) and Pasquetta (Easter Monday) are both important, as is the week leading up to them in some towns. Good Friday processions are held around the area, with a particularly impressive one on the island of Procida. Pasquetta is traditionally a day for outings and picnics to celebrate the advent of spring.

5 Saints Days
Taking place in May, September and December, the Festa di San Gennaro honours Naples' patron saint with processions of his effigy through the old quarter to the Duomo. At the Festa di San Giovanni (feast day of St John the Baptist) in June, magicians perform and locals enjoy night bathing.

6 Arts Events
Known for its museums and galleries, Naples is also home to some amazing arts events. At June's Napoli Teatro Festival *(napoliteatrofestival.it)*, the city becomes a series of pop-up theatres, while July's Amalfi Coast Music and Arts Festival *(amalfi-festival. org)* sees musicians and artists gather for events inspired by Italy's beauty.

7 Sounds of Music
The region reverberates with music throughout the year. On 21 June, free music concerts are held throughout Naples for the Festa della Musica

**Good Friday procession
in Procida**

(festadellamusicaitalia.it). Meanwhile, classical music fans head to Ravello from July to September for the Ravello Festival (ravellofestival.com). In the first week of August, Anacapri hosts the International Folklore Festival.

8 Foodie Festivals

As one of Italy's gastronomic capitals (and the birthplace of pizza), Naples is bursting with culinary festivals. Snack on freshly made pizzas at the popular Pizza Village (pizzavillage.it) in June and September, or head to the Amalfi Coast's Gusta Minori festival (gustaminori.it) at the end of the summer to devour seafood and sip on *limoncello*.

9 Sporting Events

The region offers plenty to do if you fancy getting active, from competing in the Naples Half-Marathon in February, which takes runners through the historic centre, to taking a two-wheeled tour of the city at the Napoli Bike Festival (napolibikefestival.it) in September.

10 Christmas

Decked with lights and bursting with festive markets, Naples looks splendid at Christmas. The streets around San Gregorio Armeno (*p86*) are full of locals shopping for items to complete their traditional *presepi* (nativity scenes) and concerts take place in the churches.

Traditional Neapolitan *presepio,* or nativity scene, at Christmas

---

TOP 10
SMALL CELEBRATIONS

1. O Cippo 'e Sant'Antuono
Jan
Locals light bonfires in Piazza Mercato and burn old belongings to start the new year afresh.

2. Festa Della Tammorra, Somma Vesuviana
Jun
Music and dancing to honour the *tammorra* (a traditional instrument).

3. Festa di Sant'Anna, Ischia
Jun
Elaborately decorated floats parade across the water beneath the Castello Aragonese.

4. Notte Delle Lampare, Cetara
Jul
A procession honours the role of *lampare* (lamps) in anchovy fishing.

5. Luminaria di San Domenico, Praiano
Aug
Thousands of glowing candles twinkle on streets and the Piazza San Gennaro.

6. Festa della Sfogliatella Santarosa, Conca dei Marini
Aug
A festival dedicated to local icon the *sfogliatella*, a shell-shaped pastry.

7. La Notte di San Lorenzo
10 Aug
Locals wish upon shooting stars during the annual Perseid meteor shower.

8. Capodanno Bizantino, Amalfi
Aug–Sep
Costumed parades and medieval tournaments ring in the Byzantine New Year.

9. Festa Della Castagna, Scala
Oct
Enjoy various chestnut-based delicacies at this festival, which celebrates the chestnut harvest.

10. Sagra Dei Funghi, San Giuseppe Vesuviano
Nov
The humble funghi is the guest of honour at this quirky local festival.

NIGHTS OUT

1 Enjoy an Aperitivo
Start the night the Neapolitan way, by relaxing over an aperitivo, whether it's a negroni, prosecco or a refreshing glass of vino rosso. Piazza Bellini (p84) is the perfect place to enjoy your drink, with a lively atmosphere and numerous bars offering cocktails and nibbles.

2 Lungomare Passeggiata
Join the locals on their evening *passeggiata* with a stroll along the Lungomare Caracciolo. This seafront promenade stretches along Via Partenope and Via Caracciolo, with views out across the bay to Mount Vesuvius. On one side, the calming tides; on the other, one of Naples few green areas, the leafy Villa Comunale. A blissful way to spend the evening.

3 Sunset Views Over Belvedere San Martino
Take the stairway from the centre or a Metro to Vanvitelli then walk up to Belvedere San Martino on the top of Vomero hill, near Castel Sant'Elmo and the Certosa di San Martino. This is the best spot to take in a panoramic view across the city at sunset, as the chaotic hum of the streets falls away and the twinkling lights of Spaccanapoli lie before the shadow of Mount Vesuvius.

4 Beach Clubs
The beach clubs of southern Italy take on a different hue by night. Bagnoli, Naples' westernmost *quartiere*, is home to some of the liveliest spots, including Arenile di Bagnoli (areniledibagnoli.it). Expect bars, open-air dancefloors, DJs and live bands playing until the small hours.

5 Clubbing in Capri
The clubs and tavernas of Capri come alive after midnight. Night owls should start at the Piazzetta, the social hub of the island, before heading to nearby clubs like the legendary Anema e Core (anemaecore.com/en). Many clubs host live music and revellers sing along to Neapolitan classics.

6 Vomero Pubs
On a hilltop accessed by funicular or a steady climb, Vomero is a place to let loose in the evening, with an

intriguing mix of Neapolitan nightlife and British pub culture. The hill's many pubs come to life when local football team SSC Napoli are playing, with *Gli Azzurri* (the Blues) supporters flocking to popular spots like the L'Oca Nera (*locanerairishpub.eatbu.com*) or Frank Malone (*frankmalonebrewstore.com*).

7 Listen to Jazz
Italian jazz owes as much to opera and Neapolitan folk as it does to the blues, and the city has produced unique and beloved icons like Pino Daniele. Check out the thriving jazz scene at Bourbon Street Napoli, the oldest jazz club in Naples (*bourbonstreetjazzclub.com*).

8 Teatro di San Carlo
For a cultured evening, there are few better places to visit than Europe's oldest opera house (*p94*). The horseshoe-shaped auditorium oozes 19th-century opulence with its resplendent red and gold interior and ornately frescoed ceiling. Lavishly dressed theatregoers are usually there to see and be seen.

9 Hotel Rooftops
Many of the hotels in Naples have rooftop terraces where visitors can watch the sunset with a drink in hand. Look out over the city from the swanky Sky Lounge at the Vesuvio (*vesuvio.it/en/bar*) or La Terrazza at the Romeo (*theromeocollection.com/en/romeo-napoli/restaurants-bars/la-terrazza*).

10 Spritz Culture
Few cities celebrate the Italian spritz quite like Naples. Dotted around the centre are small bars and pop-ups serving Aperol, Campari or *Limoncello* spritz for dangerously cheap prices. Cammarotta Spritz (*cammarotaspritz.it*) is perhaps the best, with locals and tourists alike congregating outside the bar from 4pm.

Piazzetta di Capri, the hub of the island's social life

TOP 10
BARS IN NAPLES

Tables outside Libreria Berisio

1. Kestè
🅶 H5 🏠 Via S. Giovanni Maggiore Pignatelli 26/27
A bar and gallery, with live jazz.

2. Libreria Berisio
🅶 N2 🏠 Via Port'Alba 28
Relax in this bookshop with a café-bar, which hosts weekend jazz.

3. L'Antiquario
🅶 M6 🏠 Via Vannella Gaetani 2
Like an elegant speakeasy, this cocktail bar has a retro feel.

4. Caffè Letterario Intra Moenia
🅶 N2 🏠 Piazza Bellini 67/70
A bookstore café favoured by students and local artists.

5. Mater
🅶 M1 🏠 Piazzetta Materdei 4
Lively wine bar running open mic nights for poets and singers.

6. Archeobar
🅶 N2 🏠 Via Mezzocannone 101
This great bar specializes in negronis.

7. Ianieri Wine
🅶 M6 🏠 Via Monte di Dio 48
A wine bar and shop selling local wines and offering tasting sessions.

8. Caseari Cautero
🅶 M1 🏠 Piazzetta Pontecorvo
Quality wine, cheese and salumi shop with some outside seating.

9. Indovino
🅶 N2 🏠 Vico Latilla 9
Natural wines, craft beers, salumi and cheese attract an arty crowd.

10. Antica Cantina Sepe
🅶 P1 🏠 Via Vergini 55
Owner Francesco Sepe hosts an epic Thursday night street party.

AREA BY AREA

The historic centre of Naples

SPACCANAPOLI TO CAPODIMONTE

The ancient heart of the city is celebrated for its striking juxtaposition of chaos and consummate artistry, but most of all for the sheer, boundless energy of the Neapolitan spirit. In many ways, this part of the city is ruled by its past (which has included innumerable disasters), but renewed investment has also allowed the area to look to the future. Narrow streets are much safer and cleaner than before and its erstwhile dilapidated, shut-away treasures are now restored and far better organized, without losing any of their uniquely vibrant feeling. Spaccanapoli is the colloquial name for the long, narrow street that runs from Via Duomo to Via Monteoliveto and is the remnant of an ancient Greco-Roman thoroughfare. The historic street now exudes a timeless charm, inviting visitors to wander through its winding lanes to discover hidden gems.

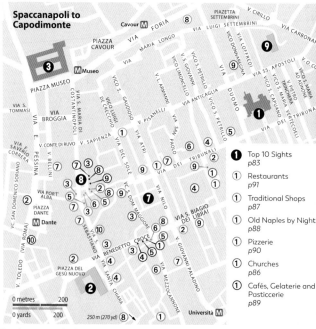

Spaccanapoli to Capodimonte

1	Top 10 Sights *p83*
1	Restaurants *p91*
1	Traditional Shops *p87*
1	Old Naples by Night *p88*
1	Pizzerie *p90*
1	Churches *p86*
1	Cafés, Gelaterie and Pasticcerie *p89*

For places to stay in this area, see p130

**Splendid divine art
in the Duomo**

abounds in the main church and its
chapels, including the huge work
dedicated to the city's patron saint,
Gennaro (Januarius).

1 Duomo

Although its position in the
present-day street-plan seems to
be an afterthought and the Neo-
Gothic façade appears perfunctory,
inside Naples' cathedral (p26) is a
fascinating treasure trove of history,
art and culture. There are ancient
remains of the Greek and Roman
cities to explore, including some
beautiful Paleo-Christian mosaics
in the baptistry, and splendid art

2 Santa Chiara

🔲 N3 🔲 Via Santa Chiara 49c
🔲 Church & cloisters: 9:30am–
5pm Mon–Sat, 10am–2pm Sun
🔲 monasterodisantachiara.it 🔳

The façade of this structure,
rebuilt after World War II, is like
a huge cliff of buff-coloured tufa,
relieved only by its portico and
giant rose window. Only the base
of its 14th-century bell tower is
original. Inside the decor has been
returned to its Gothic origins, since
all the Baroque embellishment was
destroyed in wartime bombings.
The tomb of Robert of Anjou is
the largest funerary monument
of medieval Italy, and behind this
is the delightful tiled cloister.

3 Museo Archeologico

One of the most important
museums of ancient art in the world,
Museo Archeologico (p28) houses some
of the most famous statues from
the Greco-Roman past, such as the
Callipygean Venus that set standards
of physical beauty that have endured
through the ages. Other monumental
marble works include the Farnese
Hercules, but the collec-
tions also feature
carved semi-
precious
stone, bronzes,
mosaics,
frescoes,
glassware,
Greek
vases and
Egyptian
mummies.

**Statue, Museo
Archeologico**

*Real Bosco di
Capodimonte*

North Naples

Capodimonte **5**

APODIMONTE

A56

VERGINI

Orto
Botanico **10**

Palazzo dello
Spagnolo

OCATA **6**

San Giovanni
a Carbonara **4**

Area of *Spaccanapoli to
Capodimonte* map

Ⓜ Museo **10**

10

Ⓜ Dante

Garibaldi Ⓜ

Napoli
Centrale

8 2

Porta
Nolana

10

5

Università Ⓜ

6 10

Ⓜ Toledo

*Gulf of
Naples*

Ⓜ Municipio

usteo

FERDINANDO

| 0 metres | 800 |
| 0 yards | 800 |

4 San Giovanni a Carbonara

Q1 ◮ Via Carbonara 5
⏰ 9am–6pm Mon–Sat

This 14th-century church has no façade of its own but is reached by a double staircase through a courtyard to the left of the Chapel of Santa Monica. Inside is a circular chapel with 15th-century frescoes and bas-reliefs by Spanish masters Bartolomé Ordoñez and Diego de Siloe.

5 Museo di Capodimonte

This royal palace (p32) is home to important works by some of the greatest masters, including Botticelli, Filippino Lippi, Mantegna, Bellini, Fra' Bartolomeo, Michelangelo, Raphael, Titian, Rembrandt and Dürer, as well as by every great painter working in Naples during the 17th and 18th centuries, including Caravaggio and Vivarini.

6 Palazzo dello Spagnolo

P1 ◮ Via Vergini 191

Dating from 1728, this palace offers a fine example of a well-known Neapolitan architectural element, the staircase "ad ali di falco" (with falcon wings). Separating two courtyards, the external stairway has double flights of steps with tiers of archways, a trademark of its designer, Ferdinando Sanfelice. Stucco designs can be seen throughout and attention to detail is evident above doorways.

THE THREE GUGLIE

The area's three *guglie* ("needles" or "spires") imitate the original towering contraptions built in the 1600s and 1700s to celebrate feast days. The first stone *guglia* was raised to San Gennaro, when the saint supposedly saved Naples from Vesuvius's fury in 1631. The next was dedicated to San Domenico for ending the 1656 plague. The last adorns Piazza del Gesù.

---

7 Sansevero Chapel

P2 ◮ Via Francesco de Sanctis 19/20 ⏰ 9am–7pm Wed–Sun
🌐 museosansevero.it

Designed by the 18th-century prince Raimondo di Sangro, this family chapel is full of allegorical symbolism. The statuary are among Naples' most famous, particularly the "veiled" figures of Christ and Modesty. Don't miss the Anatomical Machines. It is advisable to book your visit in advance.

8 Piazza Bellini

N2

This plaza (p52) is lined with cafés, bookshops and palaces. Of particular note is the monastery of Sant'Antonio a Port'Alba, incorporating 15th-century

Sculptures inside San
Giovanni a Carbonara

Palazzo Conca. At the centre of the
piazza, in addition to a statue of the
eponymous composer, is an archaeological excavation, revealing 5th-century
BCE Greek walls of large tufa blocks.

9 Santi Apostoli

🗹 P1 🏛 Largo Santi Apostoli 9
🕘 9:30am–1:30pm & 4:30–7pm daily

The original church is believed to have
been built in the 5th century over a
Roman temple to Mercury. Rebuilt
in the 17th century, with decoration
added over the next 100 years, the Santi
Apostoli has 17th- and 18th-century art
by Neapolitan artists as well as some of
the greatest masters of the day. Most
famous is the fresco cycle by Lanfranco,
with a trompe-l'oeil architectural setting
by Codazzi. Another highlight is the altar
that was designed by Borromini.

10 Orto Botanica

🗹 K1 🏛 Via Floria 223 🕘 9am–
2pm Mon, Wed & Fri; 9am–4pm Tue &
Thu 🌐 ortobotaniconapoli.it

Created in 1807, this botanical garden
is one of Italy's most important and
has cultivated samples of nearly all of
the world's plants and flowers. Historic
structures include the Neo-Classical
Serra Temperata, built in 1807 and the
double stairway entrance to the grounds.

**Lush greenery at the
impressive Orto Botanico**

A MORNING AT OLD
NAPLES' CHURCHES

Morning

Begin your tour of Naples' two
oldest main streets at **Piazza
del Gesù Nuovo**, where you can
admire the Guglia dell'Immacolata
and the rusticated façade of the
Gesù Nuovo (p86). Further along,
enter **Santa Chiara** (p70) to view
the medieval tombs and then go
around the back to see the
famous tiled cloister.

Stop for a drink at one
of the cafés in **Piazza San
Domenico**, where the Guglia di
San Domenico has mermaids
sculpted on its base. Across the
street, stop by at the church of
Sant'Angelo a Nilo (p86) to see
its Donatello bas-relief, and at
the next corner, look for the
ancient statue of the god of the
Nile, known familiarly as "The
Body of Naples". Follow the street
all the way to **Via Duomo**.

Next, visit the iconic **Duomo** (p26),
topped by the earliest *guglia*, and
adorned with a statue of San
Gennaro. Behind the cathedral,
discover Caravaggio's revolution-
ary painting *The Seven Acts of
Mercy* in the **Pio Monte della
Misericordia** (p71). Double back
along **Via dei Tribunali**, where you
will find more churches such as
San Gregorio Armeno (p86) and
**Santa Maria delle Anime del
Purgatorio ad Arco** (p86).

Head to **Piazza Bellini** for a drink
or a full meal at one of the cafés.

Churches

1. San Lorenzo Maggiore
⌖ P2 ⌂ Piazzetta San Gaetano 316
⌚ 9:30am–5:30pm daily
One of Naples' oldest monuments, the church is a mix of Gothic and Baroque styles.

2. Gesù Nuovo
⌖ N3 ⌂ Piazza del Gesù Nuovo 2
⌚ 9:30am–1pm & 4–7:30pm daily
The wall of this church dates back to a 15th-century fortified palace. Inside are works of art from the 16th to 19th centuries.

3. San Domenico Maggiore
⌖ N2 ⌂ Piazza San Domenico Maggiore 8a ⌚ 10am–6pm daily
Highlights at this 13th-century church include frescoes by Pietro Cavallini.

4. San Gregorio Armeno
⌖ P2 ⌂ Via S Gregorio Armeno 1
⌚ 9am–noon daily (to 1pm Sat & Sun)
San Gregorio Armeno is best known for the cult of St Patricia, whose blood "liquefies" each Tuesday.

5. Sant'Angelo a Nilo
⌖ P2 ⌂ Piazzetta Nilo ⌚ 9am–1pm daily; also 4:30–7pm Mon–Sat
This 14th-century church houses the exquisite *Assumption of the Virgin* by Renaissance artist Donatello.

6. San Paolo Maggiore
⌖ P2 ⌂ Piazza S Gaetano 76
⌚ 9am–5:30pm daily (to 1:30pm Sun)
The 8th-century church features an annexed sanctuary.

7. Santa Maria delle Anime del Purgatorio ad Arco
⌖ P2 ⌂ Via dei Tribunali 39
⌚ 10am–5pm daily (to 2pm Sun)
Bronze skulls adorn the railings outside this church.

8. San Pietro a Majella
⌖ N2 ⌂ Piazza Luigi Miraglia 393
⌚ 9am–noon & 4–6pm daily
This church was originally built in the 14th century, then restored in the 1900s.

9. Santa Maria di Donnaregina Nuova and Vecchia
⌖ P1 ⌂ Largo Donnaregina ⌚ 9:30am–4:30pm Wed–Mon (to 2pm Sun) ⌖
These Gothic and Baroque churches have been converted into a museum.

10. Santa Maria del Carmine
⌖ R3 ⌂ Piazza del Carmine 2
⌚ 7am–12:30pm & 5–7:30pm daily
Home to the Madonna Bruna icon, the focus of a Naples cult.

Façade of Sant'Angelo a Nilo with bronze sculptures

Traditional Shops

1. Di Virgilio
P2 **Via San Gregorio Armeno
18/20/43** **divirgilioart.com**
This family-run shop packs an array of
intricate terracotta figures – everything
from Pulcinella to famous footballers.

2. Luca Talarico Leather Craft
N3 **Via Domenico Capitelli 8**
lucatalarico.com
A dedicated umbrella-maker,
Giovanni Talarico opened this shop
in 1924 as he wanted to combine his
love for art with leatherwork. Today,
his grandson Luca and his wife Maria
create unique handmade leather bags,
wallets, accessories and paintings.

3. Melinoi
N3 **Via B Croce 34**
An upmarket outlet for stylish clothing,
which includes a comprehensive range
of choice designer labels from Italy,
France as well as Spain.

4. Arte in Movimento De Maria
P2 **Vico Giuseppe Maffei 3**
arteinmovimentodemaria.it
Head to this *bottega* (workshop) to
see artisans create nativity figures
and personalized figurines.

5. Colonnese
N2 **Via San Pietro a Majella 32–33**
This is one of Naples' most interesting
bookstores. You will find a good stock
of rare 18th- and 19th-century books.

6. Buccino Collection
N3 **Via Benedetto Croce 51**
buccinocollection.it
This store reproduces Capodimonte
porcelain, and other ceramic art from
Naples' illustrious past. These creatively
made pieces make for great souvenirs.

7. Via San Sebastiano Shops
N2
Along this street, just off Piazza
Bellini, you'll find Neapolitan musical

Terracotta statues for sale at
Di Virgilio

instruments, from mandolins to
the triccaballacca (a three-pronged
clacker with cymbals attached).

8. Tattoo Records
P2 **Piazzetta Nilo 15**
In an appealing little piazza
located just off Spaccanapoli,
this funky music shop is a must-
stop if you're looking for CDs of
local music or rare imports. The
proprietor will help you find everything from traditional tarantella
music to the latest Neapolitan rockers.

9. Cosmos
P2 **Via San Gregorio Armeno 5**
cosmosangregorioarmeno.com
One of the most inviting shops along
this busy shopping street, Cosmos is
packed with jewellery, souvenir-sized
lucky charms, Pulcinella figures,
decorative masks and magnets.

10. Scriptura
N2 **Via San Sebastiano 45**
scripturapelletteria.it
This small shop sells handmade
leather products, including high-
quality bags, wallets and diaries.
The beautifully packaged items
make great gifts to take home.

Old Naples by Night

Outdoor seating at the lively Kestè bar

1. Kestè
P3 Largo S Giovanni Maggiore 26
This energetic bar is open every evening for cocktails and beers. It attracts a student crowd that is drawn by Kestè's pocket-friendly prices and regular art and photography shows.

2. Perditempo
N2 Via San Pietro a Majella 8
An intimate bar-bookshop-music store, located in the historic part of Naples, this is anything but a "waste of time" as its name might suggest. An eclectic music soundtrack accompanies the stimulating conversation and good drinks.

3. Caffè dell'Epoca
N3 Via Santa Maria di Costantinopoli 82/83
Caffè dell'Epoca is a tiny place with a few tables along the street. A low-key café by day, it transforms into one of Piazza Bellini's most popular drinking holes in the evening.

4. L'Antiquario
L6 Via Vannella Gaetani 2
The Art-Nouveau-inspired L'Antiquario is renowned for its award-winning mixologists. There's live jazz every Wednesday night.

5. Vineria San Sebastiano
N1 Piazza Bellini 72 Sun
A local favourite for an aperitivo, this wine bar offers a selection of wines, craft beers and liqueurs, as well as tasty traditional snacks including vegan and vegetarian options.

6. Archeobar
N2 Via Mezzocannone 101/Bis Tue
This cosy cocktail bar is the perfect place to mingle with the locals. It has a wide selection of drinks, and an even better collection of books in its upstairs library. Pick up a new tome or kick back and enjoy one of the bar's frequent gig nights.

7. Bourbon Street
N2 Via Bellini 52/53 Mon
This large jazz club features local talent every evening. In summer Bourbon Street organizes jazz cruises around the bay.

8. Mamamù
P3 Via Sedile Di Porto 46 Sun–Wed
A cosy live music venue, this is a hot spot for the young music scene, which showcases indie rock, punk and electric music. Mamamù is frequented by local talents and it organizes DJ sets and karaoke nights, which are quite popular.

9. Pepi Vintage Room
N2 Vico San Domenico Maggiore 23
Casual bar that spills into a narrow alley just below Piazza Luigi Miraglia, with friendly bar staff and creative cocktails. Oddly, they also sell sunglasses.

10. Berisio
N2 Via Port'Alba 28/29
Established in 1956, this captivating wine bar has vintage, new, old and used books lining the walls. On weekends there is live jazz and blues.

Cafés, Gelaterie and Pasticcerie

1. Gran Caffè Neapolis
N2 **Piazza S Domenico Maggiore 14/15**
This café offers a good range of savoury snacks, breakfast fare and is great for cocktails in the evening.

2. Bar Mexico
N2 **Piazza Dante 86**
Bar Mexico is reputed to have the best espresso in town. Those who don't want it sweetened (*alla napoletana*) can ask for a *caffè amaro* (bitter coffee). A hot-weather winner is the *frappe di caffè* (iced whipped coffee). You can also stock up on some coffee blends to take home.

3. Spazio Nea
N2 **Via Costantinopoli 53**
Located just steps from Piazza Bellini, this contemporary gallery is a gathering spot for artistic types. There's indoor and outdoor seating areas at the lovely café. They also host theatre, performances and special events.

4. Gay-Odin
N3 **Via B Croce 6**
A Naples institution that is a paradise for chocolate lovers. Try the hot chocolate or the divine ice cream.

5. Scaturchio
N2 **Piazza S Domenico Maggiore 19**
The wonderful traditional pastries on offer here are noted all over Naples; it's a real treat to sample the wares while checking out this piazza. Don't arrive too late or they might have sold out.

6. Pasticceria Mennella
N3 **Via Toledo 110**
This 40-year-old gelaterie (ice-cream parlour) chain specializes in making gelato from fresh, local produce such as nuts from Sorrento and apricots from Vesuvius.

7. Intra Moenia
N2 **Piazza Bellini 70**
A good place to hang out and enjoy a drink. In warm weather it's also a lively LGBTQ+ venue in the evenings.

8. Caffè Arabo
N2 **Piazza Bellini 64**
Not just a great café, but a purveyor of tasty Arabic goodies and full meals.

9. Bar Lemme Lemme
N2 **Piazza Bellini 74**
Another vantage point in Piazza Bellini for an aperol spritz and snacks, while there's a small art gallery on-site.

10. Leopoldo Infante
N2 **Toledo 8**
This café and bar is a great place for coffee, traditional Neapolitan cakes and ice cream all year round.

Patrons enjoying the desserts at Leopoldo Infante

Pizzerie

Pizza maker serving pizzas at Pizzeria Sorbillo

1. Pizzeria Sorbillo
🅟 N2 🅐 Via dei Tribunali 32
🅦 sorbillo.it 🅒 Sun · €€
The main restaurant is modern but the stand-up branch next door dates from 1935. Pizza makers here twirl the dough, dash on the topping and pop it into the brick oven. Wait times can be long.

2. L'Antica Pizzeria "da Michele"
🅟 Q2 🅐 Via Cesare Sersale 1
🅒 081 553 92 04 · €
The menu at this traditional *pizzerie* is limited to only four varieties of pizza, *margherita, marinara, cosacca and marita*. The wait is often considerable and tables are shared.

3. Lombardi a Santa Chiara
🅟 N3 🅐 Via B Croce 59
🅒 081 552 07 80 · €
Follow the locals downstairs to eat fresh pizza while standing or sitting on stools.

4. Di Matteo
🅟 P2 🅐 Via dei Tribunali 94
🅦 pizzeriadimatteo.it 🅒 Sun · €
As well as pizza, try some *frittura* here – deep-fried titbits of vegetables, rice and cheese.

5. Pizzeria Dal Presidente
🅟 P2 🅐 Via dei Tribunali 120
🅒 081 296 710 · €
Another pizzeria on this busy street, which gained its moment of fame when then US President Bill Clinton stopped by for a snack.

6. Pizzeria Starita
🅟 M1 🅐 Via Materdei 27/28
🅦 pizzeriestarita.it 🅒 Mon · €
One of the oldest *pizzerie* in Naples, this place is famous for its *antipasti* and fresh pizzas. The *angioletti fritti* (fried angels) are a popular item, too. Expect a queue, especially at weekends.

7. Antica Pizzeria Port'Alba
🅟 N2 🅐 Via Port'Alba 18 🅦 antica pizzeriaportalba.com 🅒 Tue · €€
Through an archway off Piazza Dante, this pizzeria even has a traditional wood-fired oven with lava stones from Mount Vesuvius.

8. Pizzeria Trianon da Ciro
🅟 Q2 🅐 Via Pietro Colletta 44
🅒 081 553 94 26 · €
Taking its name from a famous theatre and every bit as traditional as "da Michele" – just across the street – this eatery is more upmarket, with a larger choice. The decor recalls the city's belle époque heyday.

9. Pizzeria Vesi
🅟 P2 🅐 Via S. Biagio dei Librai 115
🅒 081 55110 35 · €
Pizzeria Vesi specializes in "pizza DOC" – a delicious aromatic union of mozzarella balls, pomodorini (cherry tomatoes) and basil.

10. Antica Pizzeria da Gaetano
🅟 R1 🅐 Via Casanova 109
🅒 081 554 54 30 🅒 Sun · €
Fresh produce cooked in a wood oven and friendly staff make this a popular hangout spot.

Restaurants

1. La Cantina della Sapienza
N2 ⌂Via Sapienza 40
☏081 45 90 78 ⌚Tue & Wed · €
The menu changes daily here. Dishes such as *melanzane alla parmigiana* (aubergine with mozzarella and tomato) make a regular appearance.

2. La Cantina del Sole
P3 ⌂Via G Paladino 3 ☏081 552 73 12 ⌚Mon · €€
A local favourite, this restaurant is noted for recipes that date back to the 1600s.

3. Bellini
N2 ⌂Via Santa Maria di Costantinopoli 79–80
☏081 45 97 74 · €€
This *trattoria* specializes in seafood pasta and grilled catch of the day. Pizza also available.

4. La Taverna a Santa Chiara
N3 ⌂Via Santa Chiara 6
☏081 048 49 08 ⌚Sun · €€€
Relish quality traditional food here, including homemade pasta such as *spaghetti con soffritto* (sautéed spaghetti).

5. Biancomangiare
M3 ⌂Vico S Nicola alla Carità 13/14
☏081 552 02 26 ⌚Sun D · €€
Taking full advantage of its location next to the market, this family cantina serves fresh fish at great prices.

6. Un Sorriso Integrale
N2 ⌂Vico S Pietro a Maiella 6
☏081 455 026 · €
This vegetarian café serves fresh, healthy meals, including a selection of sharing plates.

7. Neapolis Specialità Greche
P3 ⌂Via Giovanni Paladino 22
☏081 551 55 84 · €
Cheap and tasty Greek dishes include kebabs and filled pitta breads.

8. Lombardi 1892
P1 ⌂Via Foria 12/14
☏081 45 62 20 ⌚Mon · €€
A popular (but, thankfully, rarely crowded) restaurant and pizzeria with a wonderful antipasto buffet that features seasonal delicacies.

9. La Locanda del Grifo
N2 ⌂Via Francesco del Giudice 14 ☏081 557 14 92 · €
This *trattoria* and pizzeria serves Neapolitan fare made using seasonal produce. The pretty patio overlooks a medieval campanile.

10. Mimì alla Ferrovia
R1 ⌂Via Alfonso d'Aragona 19–21 ☏081 553 85 25 ⌚Sun · €€
Mimì specializes in fish and seafood. but they also have great *pasta e ceci* (soup with chickpeas).

Delicious seafood dish at
Mimì alla Ferrovia

TOLEDO TO CHIAIA

The area known as "Royal Naples" is notably more spacious and open than the narrow streets of Spaccanapoli. Elegant architecture from various ages graces the terrain here, which is also home to one of the oldest neighbourhoods, maritime Santa Lucia. Above it all, the Vomero district has a fine castle and monastery overlooking the bay and one of the city's best parks. To the west is the Mergellina district, with its working port and busy restaurants lined up along the coast.

1 Palazzo Reale
The Royal Palace *(p22)* is largely 18th-century in character, with its vast layout, imposing façade and important rooms such as the ballroom and the chapel. Later embellishments took a Neo-Classical turn, in particular the grand staircase. Under Napoleonic rule many of the rooms received a make-over, which dominates the decor today. Don't miss the fine Renaissance and Baroque paintings from the royal collection, including works by Guercino, Spadarino and several Flemish masters.

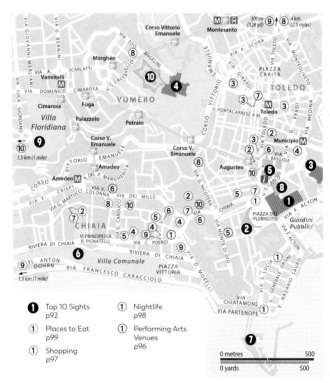

1 Top 10 Sights p92	**1** Nightlife p98		
1 Places to Eat p99	**1** Performing Arts Venues p96		
1 Shopping p97			

0 metres 500
0 yards 500

For places to stay in this area, see p130

San Francesco di Paola on Piazza del Plebiscito

2 San Francesco di Paola
M6 Piazza del Plebiscito
6:45am–noon & 4:30–7:30pm
Mon–Sat, 8am–noon Sun

The impetus to build this facsimile of the Pantheon came from the Napoleonic king Joachim Murat (1808–15). Completed under the reinstated Bourbon dynasty, the idea was to do away with the chaotic jumble around the palace by recreating a version of the ancient Roman temple to the gods and setting it off with arcades echoing those of St Peter's. It dominates a semicircular piazza with the Palazzo Reale at the opposite end.

3 Castel Nuovo
This rather sombre fortress (p24) is a study in stylistic contrasts – in direct opposition to its bulky grey towers, the marble Triumphal Arch exudes the delicacy of the early Renaissance. Inside, its rooms allow visitors to peel back the layers of history that helped define the city. The spartan blankness is relieved by the ceiling of the Barons' Hall, while the fresco fragments and sculptures in the chapel juxtapose with the harsh reality of the dungeons. In addition, there are fine collections of religious and secular artwork. Go up to the battlements to see the panorama.

4 Certosa e Museo di San Martino
If there is one place that could be called the true museum (p34) of Naples, this former monastery takes that spot. All aspects of the city's history and cultural output seem to be represented here through the varied collections and diverse architecture. These include a large collection of Nativity scenes, some of Naples' most significant paintings and sculptures, views of the city painted in different eras, a decorative arts collection, and the exuberantly Baroque church, decorated by the best Neapolitan artists of the 17th and 18th centuries.

Stunning Baroque interior of the Certosa di San Martino

5 Galleria Umberto I
N5 **Main entrance on Via San Carlo**

Part of the urban renewal plan following the cholera epidemic of 1884, this space is home to buildings with Neo-Renaissance embellishments and marble floors, overarched by a roof of iron and glass. Located across from the Royal Palace and Teatro di San Carlo, the spot became popular with the city's smart and artistic set, and even today has an air of bygone charm.

6 Villa Comunale
K6 **Via Caracciolo**
May–Oct: 7am–midnight daily; Nov–Apr: 7am–10pm daily

Designed by Luigi Vanvitelli and inaugurated in 1781 as the royal gardens, this public park is on the bay. It had 19th-century copies of Classical statuary, and was once home to the ancient Farnese Bull group, now in the Museo Archeologico (p28). Other adornments include a Neo-Classical aquarium; an iron-and-glass bandstand and a zoological station with a turtle rescue centre.

7 Castel dell'Ovo
M6 **Via Partenope**

In ancient times, this spot was part of the vast estate of the Roman general Lucullus. At the end of the 5th century an order of monks founded a monastery here, then the Normans built the first castle. It was modified by succeeding dynasties, achieving its present form in the 16th century. Legend has it that its name derives from a hidden magic egg (uovo), supposedly placed there by the Roman poet Virgil. The building is temporarily closed for renovation but is still worth seeing from the outside.

8 Teatro di San Carlo
N5 **Via San Carlo 98F**
10am–1:30pm & 2–5:30pm daily (subject to stage activities)

Built by order of King Charles, this opera house predates the La Scala in Milan by some 40 years. Officially

---

THE BIRTH OF GRAND OPERA

Along with its many other musical accomplishments, Italy is the home of opera. Inspired by Classical Greek drama, the first opera was composed by northerner Monteverdi towards the end of the 16th century. But it was Naples, renowned for its inimitable castrati (p59), who made the genre its own. The accompanying sets, costumes and dance were refined, and the whole art form soon went international.

Gilded interior of the Teatro di San Carlo

opened on 4 November 1737, it is one of the most important opera houses in the world. The interior was originally in the Bourbon colours (silver, gold and sky blue), but after being rebuilt following a fire in 1816 the colour scheme is now mostly gold and red, though no less sumptuous. The theatre contains a museum charting its history.

9 Museo Nazionale della Ceramica Duca di Martina

◪ J4 ◪ Villa Floridiana, Via Cimarosa 77 ◪ 9:30am–5pm Wed–Mon
ⓦ museiitaliani.it ◪

Since 1927 this villa has been home to a collection of European and Oriental decorative art donated by the Duke of Martina. It showcases a diverse array of exquisite artifacts, stunning paintings, intricate sculptures and ornate furnishings.

10 Castel Sant'Elmo

◪ L4 ◪ Via Tito Angelini
◪ Castle: 8:30am–7:30pm daily; museum: 9:30am–5pm Wed–Mon ◪

This Angevin castle dating from 1329 was upgraded to its six-point configuration in the 16th century, giving it a militaristic presence looming above the city. It now houses libraries, cultural activities and exhibitions.

Colourful boats and yachts moored outside the Castel dell'Ovo

A DAY IN ROYAL NAPLES

Morning
Start inside **Galleria Umberto I**, where you can try one of Naples' iconic pastries at **La Sfogliatella Mary** (p99). The elegant Neo-Classical façade of the **Teatro di San Carlo** is directly across the **Via San Carlo**.

Head right and around the corner into **Piazza del Plebiscito**. You will arrive at the massive dome of the church of **San Francesco di Paola** (p93), and on your left, you will find the **Palazzo Reale** (p23). Walk towards the church, admiring the bronze equestrian statues of kings Charles III and Ferdinand I. Then retrace your steps across the piazza to the Royal Palace. Enter the courtyard and ascend the magnificent staircase up to the apartments.

Take a break for a snack or lunch at the **Gran Caffè Gambrinus** (p99), just outside the piazza.

Afternoon
Head back past the Teatro di San Carlo and the palace gardens, which feature giant statues of horse-tamers at the gate. Continue straight ahead, crossing the lawns to the **Castel Nuovo** (p24). Soak up the views from the parapets. Finally, head up **Via Medina** to the **Caffeteria de Medina**, where you can enjoy classic seafood dishes.

Performing Arts Venues

1. Associazione Scarlatti
📍 L6 🏛 Piazza dei Martiri 58
🌐 associazionescarlatti.it
The best of Naples' small musical companies, it hosts classical chamber music and the occasional jazz group. A typical evening might feature the music of Debussy, Ravel, Chausson and Frank. Venues change frequently.

2. Teatro Augusteo
📍 M5 🏛 Piazza Duca d'Aosta 263
🌐 teatroaugusteo.it
Musical comedies are a speciality at this theatre. Watch contemporary productions, in line with the centuries-old tradition of comic theatre in Naples.

3. Galleria Toledo
📍 M4 🏛 Via Concezione a Montecalvario 34 🌐 galleriatoledo.it
This modern theatre offers avant-garde local works and new international fringe and experimental plays, translated into Italian.

4. Teatro Stabile
📍 N5 🏛 Piazza Municipio 1
🌐 teatrostabilenapoli.it
Opened in 1779, this historic theatre has developed into a leading cultural centre and hosts productions touring Italy. It is known for its elegant architecture and acoustics.

5. Politeama
📍 M6 🏛 Via Monte di Dio 80
🌐 teatropoliteama.it
This large, modern space hosts productions of international music, dance and drama. Performers have included German dancer Pina Bausch and US composer Philip Glass.

6. Nuovo Sancarluccio
📍 K6 🏛 Via S Pasquale a Chiaia 49
📞 081 544 8891
Small companies gravitate here, alternating with cabaret shows. The setting is intimate and engaging.

7. Teatro Nuovo
📍 M4 🏛 Via Montecalvario 16
🌐 teatronuovonapoli.it
Fringe, experimental and the best of new international theatre are the highlights here.

8. Centro di Musica Antica Pietà de' Turchini
📍 M5 🏛 Via S Caterina da Siena 38
🌐 turchini.it
In a deconsecrated Baroque church, the Orchestra Cappella della Pietà de' Turchini performs classical music of mostly Neapolitan composers.

9. Teatro Bellini
📍 N2 🏛 Via Conte di Ruvo 14
🌐 teatrobellini.it
Bellini offers mainstream theatre, as well as international and local musicals and concerts. Productions have included *Fiddler on the Roof*.

10. Sannazaro
📍 M5 🏛 Via Chiaia 157
🌐 teatrosannazaro.it
This lovely theatre dating from 1874 features its own company, often performing works in Neapolitan dialect.

Elegant façade of the Teatro Bellini

Shopping

1. Paolo Bowinkel
◼ L6 **◻** Piazza dei Martiri 24
◻ bowinkel.it
One of Naples' finest dealers of objets d'art prints. Expect to find Italian prints that are centuries-old as well as more modern ones, and a host of other Neapolitan memorabilia.

2. Rubinacci
◼ L5 **◻** Palazzo Cellamare, Via Chiaia 149E
Naples' most exclusive tailoring services, specializing in bespoke suits and requiring appointments. They also have ready made clothes.

3. Fusaro
◼ M5 **◻** Via Toledo 276, Piazza Dante 76/77
Local chain specializing in designer gear for men – shoes, suits, shirts and ties, jeans and jackets, as well as caps, bags and belts.

4. Rebecca
◼ L6 **◻** Via Santa Caterina a Chiaia 10–11
With a presence in nearly 30 countries around the world, Rebecca offers stylish jewellery at affordable prices. Silver and gold are featured, with an emphasis on modern pieces compatible with today's taste.

5. Restauro Lepre
◼ K6 **◻** Via Carlo Poerio 80
One of Chiaia's best antique shops, Restauro Lepre has furniture, figurines and other bits and bobs all made to shine by a skillful, friendly, father-and-son duo.

6. Pietrasalata
◼ M5 **◻** Via Chiaia 184
The atelier of jeweller Valerio Pirolo, whose work is inspired by his diving adventures as a boy in the Bay of Naples, showcases his silver pieces. The rings, earrings, necklaces and

Antique prints for sale at Paolo Bowinkel

bracelets are based on marine forms such as coral, seaweed, star-fish and octopi.

7. Tramontano
◼ L5 **◻** Via Chiaia 143
Italians are known the world over for their leather goods, including bags and shoes. Traditional Neapolitan craftsmanship is the byword here.

8. Cameo De Paola
◼ L3 **◻** Via Tito Angelini 20
One of several coral and cameo shops in the vicinity that features a vast selection of pieces at highly affordable prices.

9. Antichità Ciro Guarracino
◼ L6 **◻** Via Vannella Gaetani 26
Long-time antique store near Piazza dei Martiri deals in furniture, paintings and other pieces of art from the Baroque era through to the 20th century.

10. Marinella
◼ L6 **◻** Riviera di Chiaia 287
This workshop has crafted elegant silk ties, scarves and shoes for over a century.

Nightlife

An assortment of spirits
on offer at Ba-Bar

1. S'move Light Bar
L6 Vico dei Sospiri 10A Aug
Chic and stylish venue serving
delicious cocktails, and other tipples.
Although there's no dance floor, the
excellent selection of music keeps
things moving.

2. Al Barcadero
N6 Banchina Santa Lucia 2
This bar captures the charm of the
Santa Lucia quarter, immortalized in
one of the most famous Neapolitan
songs. By the water, near Castel
dell'Ovo, it's great for hanging out
and enjoying the views.

3. Anthill
M4 Via Toledo 177
Situated on the top floor of a building
near the Piazza del Plebiscito, this
contemporary cocktail and tapas bar
attracts huge crowds. It is known for
its excellent aperitifs, which can be
enjoyed on the rooftop terrace.

4. Cammarota Spritz
M4 Vico Lungo Teatro Nuovo 31
Mon
Perhaps the most down-to-earth
bar in town, serving €1 spritz as well
as limoncello and wine. It's popular
among students and is lively at night.

5. Enoteca Belledonne
L6 Vico Belledonne
a Chiaia 18
Shelves of wine bottles lining the
walls and a rustic decor provide a
perfect backdrop for this trendy
wine bar. An extensive wine list
and light fare are on offer.

6. 66 Fusion Bar
L6 Via Bisignano 58
With an impressively stocked bar,
this nightlife spot is popular for its
inventive cocktails and lively atmosphere. Excellent wines are available
and there is an outdoor seating area.

7. Swig Chiaia
K5 Via G. Martucci 67
Mon & Tue
This welcoming bar offers creative
cocktails and uniquely flavoured
shots. Visitors are given the option of
choosing the music played at the bar.

8. Club 21
N6 Via Nazario Sauro 21B
Nightclub with a lively atmosphere
frequented by young locals and
tourists. Expect live music, jazz nights,
DJ sets and various events.

9. Ba-Bar
L6 Via Bisignano 20
For an elegant evening out, head to the
stylish Chiaia neighbourhood where
locals go for an evening *aperitivo* or
dinner and drinks. The French bistro
atmosphere, friendly service, extensive
wine list and international beer selection
make this lively night spot stand out.

10. Discoteca il Fico
J2 Via Tasso 466
A villa dating from the 1800s is the
fine setting for this chic disco bar.
During summer, the scene moves
outdoors to the terrace from where
there are great views of the Bay of
Naples and Mount Vesuvius.

Places to Eat

1. Gran Caffè Gambrinus

⬛ M5 ⬛ Via Chiaia 1 · €€

This *belle époque* institution still retains much of its original decor. It was once popular with free-thinking intellectuals and writers, and was closed down by the Fascists as a result. The pastries and buffet lunch are good.

2. Dora

⬛ J6 ⬛ Via Ferdnando Palasciano 30 ⬛ Mon · €€

A local favourite, Dora is known for its delectable seafood platters featuring the freshest catches of the day.

3. Augustus

⬛ N4 ⬛ Via Toledo 147 · €

This *pasticceria* (pastry shop) is the perfect place to procure classic signature sweets such as *sfogliatella* (sweet or creamy shell-shaped pastry) and *babà* (soft, spongy sweet dough soaked in delicious liqueur).

4. Crudore

⬛ L6 ⬛ Via Carlo Poerio, 45/46 ⬛ Mon · €€€

Situated very close to the sea, Crudore is a haven for seafood lovers. It has a modern and stylish ambience and serves some of the freshest raw fish in Naples.

5. Brandi

⬛ M5 ⬛ Salita Sant'Anna di Palazzo 1 ⬛ 081 41 69 28 ⬛ Mon · €€

A Naples institution, laying claim to having invented the pizza margherita during a visit from Italy's Queen Margherita in 1889. Full restaurant menu, too. Reservations essential.

6. LUISE Toledo

⬛ M5 ⬛ Via Toldeo 266 ⬛ 081 41 53 67 · €

A small deli offering fried food delights such as *pizza fritta*, *arancini* (fried rice balls) and a selection of pasta and meat dishes.

7. Donna Sofia a Chiaia

⬛ M5 ⬛ Via Chiaia 188 ⬛ 081 277 8201 · €

Come for the deep-fried calzone stuffed with ricotta, peppers, provola and tomato at this popular pizzeria.

8. Osteria da Tonino

⬛ K5 ⬛ Via Santa Teresa a Chiaia 47 ⬛ 081 42 15 33 ⬛ Mon D · €€

Excellent dishes at this lively spot include the delicious seafood stew.

9. Ciro a Mergellina

⬛ K2 ⬛ Via Mergellina 21 ⬛ 081 68 17 80 ⬛ Mon · €€

Superb seafood and pasta combinations at this restaurant draw a loyal following.

10. La Sfogliatella Mary

⬛ M5 ⬛ Via Galleria Umberto I 66 ⬛ Tue · €€

This is among the best places in Naples to try shell-shaped pastries.

Baked treats on offer at La Sfogliatella Mary

VESUVIUS AND AROUND

Few places on earth are as awe-inspiring as this area of southern Italy. Here you'll find the captivating Pompeii, a wealthy Roman city that has been preserved for centuries beneath the ash of the imposing Mount Vesuvius; the excavation area is now a UNESCO World Heritage Site. The town of Herculaneum, which was also preserved after the eruption of Mount Vesuvius in 79 CE, is located near Pompeii. Both archaeological sites are replete with exquisite ancient art and architecture that highlight the rich Roman heritage of the region. In the 18th century, the unearthing of the treasures of Pompeii and Herculaneum inspired kings to build sumptuous palaces near the excavation sites, so that they could sample the exciting discoveries first-hand.

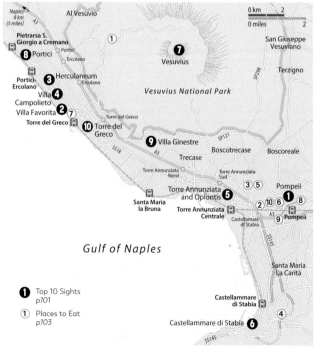

1 Top 10 Sights
p101

① Places to Eat
p103

For places to stay in this area, see p131

1 Pompeii

Discovered by accident in the 1590s, certainly no archaeological find is more important than that of ancient Pompeii *(p38)*, where a culture was captured forever by the eruption of Mount Vesuvius in 79 CE. Not only can you see the streets, buildings, art, tools, jewellery, and even the food and drink of the people who lived here, but plaster casts reveal the people themselves.

2 Villa Favorita

L2 **Corso Resina 283, Ercolano** **10am–6pm Tue–Sun**

Set in an extensive park, Villa Favorita was boarded up at least 100 years ago. With Italian Unification the noble homes became an obsolete symbol of decadence. The park and the annexe are open to visitors.

3 Herculaneum

E4 **Hours vary, chech website** **ercolano.beniculturali.it**

Originally a resort in ancient times located right on the sea, this town was buried alive by mud and lava from Vesuvius. Fortunately, wooden structures and other perishable materials were preserved under the lava. However the excavations began in the 18th century when archaeology had yet to be developed, so diggers were not very careful, being mostly on a royal treasure hunt for statuary, mosaics and fresco paintings

4 Villa Campolieto

L2 **Corso Resina 283, Ercolano** **10am–6pm Tue–Sat, 10am–1pm Sun**

This villa was designed by the Vanvittelli brothers between 1760–75. It has a circular portico, where concerts are held, and offers a lovely panorama of the bay. Some of the rooms have been restored to their original decor, while others are used for special exhibitions.

5 Torre Annunziata and Oplontis

E4 **Via Sepolcri 1** **8:30am–7:30pm daily**

Few places present such a stark contrast to the visitor as this one. The squalor of uncontrolled urban blight hides, within its depressed grime, imperial splendours of the ancient world. Two blocks from the train station lie the ruins of one of the most sumptuous villas to have been preserved by Vesuvius's eruption.

The Torre Annunziata and Oplontis complex

Castellammare di Stabia overlooking the Gulf of Naples

6 Castellammare di Stabia
E4

This port town has been known since ancient times for its thermal springs that are each thought to be therapeutic in specific ways. Nearby, the ruins of aristocratic villas, Arianna and San Marco *(p41)*, offer glimpses into wealthy lifestyles of 2,000 years ago.

7 Vesuvius
D3 **Crater: Mar & Oct: 9am–4pm daily; Apr–Sep: 9am–5pm daily; Nov–Feb: 9am–3pm daily** **parco nazionaledelvesuvio.it**

Continental Europe's only active volcano has not erupted since its last rumble in 1944, but experts say it could happen at any time; an invigorating hike around the crater is certainly a memorable experience. Today, the volcano inspires both fear and fascination and it is constantly monitored for activity. From the parking lot at the end of the road it is a 30-minute walk along a gravel path to the summit, which affords glimpses into the crater as well as magnificent views around the bay.

8 Reggia di Portici
L2 **Via Università 100, Portici** **Summer: 9:30am–7pm Tue–Sun; winter: 9am–6pm Tue–Sun** **centromusa.it**

An 18th-century *Reggia* (palace) of King Charles III and Queen Maria, designed by Antonio Medrano, this was

---

THE GOLDEN MILE

The 18th-century evolution of *Il Miglio d'Oro* can be traced back to Maria Amalia Cristina, Queen of Naples. She had grown up in a Viennese palace adorned with two marble statues unearthed at Herculaneum. When she arrived in Naples, she wanted a palace near the site. It started a trend among the nobility and some 120 villas were built.

---

the first and greatest of the Vesuvian Villas; the rest of which were built by other members of the Bourbon court. Once left in neglect, these villas have had some of their grandeur restored.

9 Villa delle Ginestre
D4 **Via Villa delle Ginestre 19, Torre del Greco** **10am–1pm Tue–Sun**

This beautiful villa was built at the end of the 17th century. It was home to 19th-century poet and philosopher Giacomo Leopardi in his later years.

10 Torre del Greco
L3

Set midway between Naples and Pompeii and just beneath the slopes of Vesuvius, this town has been home to coral and cameo artisans for centuries, a craft that still draws admirers today.

Places to Eat

1. Kona, Ercolano

📍 L2 🏠 Via Osservatorio 14 📞 081 777 39 68 🕐 D Mon–Thu · €€

Surrounded by gardens and a view of the Gulf of Naples, Kona offers a tranquil dining experience. Seafood specialities and traditional pasta dishes make up the menu; the fresh seafood salad comes recommended.

2. Ristorante Suisse, Pompeii

📍 E4 🏠 Piazza Porta Marina Inferiore 10–13 📞 081 862 25 36 · €€

Of all the restaurants outside the main gate of the ruins, this one offers the best atmosphere. It has indoor and outside seating, and serves a good standard of *trattoria* fare.

3. Zi Caterina, Pompeii

📍 E4 🏠 Via Roma 20 📞 081 850 74 47 🕐 Tue · €€

Seafood is a speciality here; try *seppie con finocchi e olive* (cuttlefish with fennel and olives). The wine list features local vintages.

4. La Medusa Hotel, Castellammare di Stabia

📍 E4 🏠 Passeggiata Archeologica 5 📞 081 872 33 83 🕐 Nov–Mar · €€€

This elegant hotel has a large dining room and terrace and it offers set meals, as well as *à la carte* selections.

5. Il Ristorante Anfiteatro, Pompeii

📍 E4 🏠 Via Plinio 9 📞 081 850 60 42 🕐 Wed · €€

Located right outside the excavations, this restaurant has been running since 1922. The fresh fish is a good choice in summer.

6. Todisco, Pompeii

📍 E4 🏠 Piazzale Schettini 19 📞 081 850 50 51 🕐 Mon · €

Friendly, affordable canteen in the centre of town, offering an unforgettable dining experience.

PRICE CATEGORIES

For a three-course meal for one with half a bottle of wine (or equivalent meal), taxes and extra charges.

€ under €30 €€ €30–€50 €€€ over €50

---

7. Osteria del Porto, Torre del Greco

📍 L3 🏠 Via Spiaggia del Fronte 8 📞 081 012 53 30 🕐 Tue · €€

Seafood restaurant by the port, serving fresh catch and fine desserts.

8. Tubba Catubba, Ercolano

📍 D3 🏠 Corso Resina 302 📞 081 344 35 03 🕐 Mon · €

Situated next to the ruins, this place offers excellent homemade dishes.

9. Osteria Da Peppino, Pompeii

📍 E4 🏠 Via Duca d'Aosta 39 📞 081 850 48 21 🕐 Tue · €€

Enjoy alfresco dining under trellis draped by vines. The menu is reasonably priced.

10. President, Pompeii

📍 E4 🏠 Piazza Schettini 12 📞 081 850 72 45 🕐 Mon & Tue · €€€

Near the site of Pompeii, this Michelin-starred restaurant with an elegant dining space is run by chef Paolo Gramaglia. Gramaglia uses high quality ingredients and serves cuisine with fresh takes on traditional recipes. There's also an excellent wine list.

Elegant dining area of the President in Pompeii

THE ISLANDS, SORRENTO AND THE SOUTH

Renowned for its picture-postcard landscapes, this area features verdant-crowned cliffs plunging into the blue sea. These islands are where the Greeks first brought their high culture to the area, where Roman emperors lived in stupendous luxury, and where, in more recent times, the world's most glamorous celebrities indulged in their own lavish lifestyles. When the American writer John Steinbeck first saw the Amalfi Coast he was moved to uncontrollable weeping. He was not the first – nor will he be the last – to succumb to the emotional impact of the area's beauty.

1 Ischia

The island of Ischia is surmounted by an extinct 788-m (2,585-ft) volcano, Monte Epomeo, and the many hot mineral springs here (some of them radioactive) have drawn cure- and pleasure-seekers to their soothing sources since ancient times. The island was also the first place in the area to be colonized by the Greeks, in the 8th century BCE. Some highlights on Ischia include Giardini la Mortella, a lush

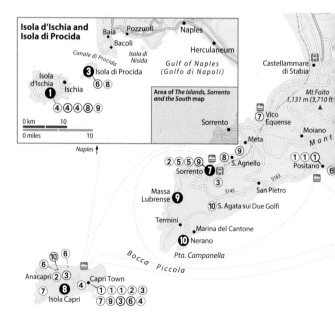

Colourful houses in the village of Sant'Angelo on Ischia

subtropical and Mediterranean garden oasis, and Baia di Sorgeto, one of the island's most popular hot springs. The series of rock pools at Sorgeto, which are heated by volcanic activity below the surface, are warm enough to swim in during the winter.

2 Paestum
These ancient Greek temples (p46) are among the most complete – and most evocative – to have made it into modern times, even taking into account those in Greece itself. Besides the beauty and majesty of these timeless architectural structures, this site has offered up countless other treasures, such as the remains of the thriving Greco-Roman city that thrived here for some 1,000 years. The wonderful on-site museum is a repository of many unique finds, including the only known Greek paintings to have survived the ravages of time. Unearthed from a tomb found nearby, the frescoes include a captivating glimpse into the past, depicting a joyous banquet of lovers and a renowned diver – possibly a metaphor for the Greek conception of the afterlife.

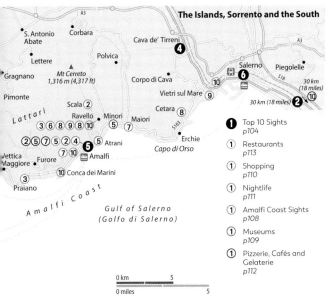

3 Procida
☑ B4

Smaller than Capri and Ischia and much less touristy, Procida attracts holiday-makers looking for tranquility and cultural tradition. The island has highly fertile soil and is noted for its lemons, considered the best in the region. The island's most original feature, however, is its unique architecture. The colourful houses along the Marina Chiaiolella, Marina Corricella and Marina di Sancio Cattolico are known for their vaults – built as winter boat shelters – arches and external staircases.

4 Cava de' Tirreni
☑ F4

In a mountainous valley situated north of the Amalfi Coast, this town was put up in the Middle Ages thanks to the Benedictine abbey Badia della Santissima Trinità (Abbey of the Holy Trinity) founded in 1011. A visit to the abbey (*badiadicava.it*) and the medieval Borgo Scacciaventi in the town's centre is an evocative walk through time.

5 Amalfi Coast
☑ E5

The famed Costiera Amalfitana lives up to the highest expectations. The winding corniche road offers striking panoramas, and some of the towns seem to defy gravity, clinging to steep slopes. Beauty and history are everywhere, with the most pop-ular destinations being the towns of Amalfi, Positano and Ravello (*p44*). The beaches are rocky yet undeniably beautiful, and time spent discovering this perpendicular paradise never fails to delight.

6 Salerno
☑ F4

Though the city is often ignored by the tourism industry, extensive restoration work on the historic centre has ignited some interest. The Romanesque Duomo on Piazza Alfano I is a reminder that Salerno was the capital of southern Italy in the 11th century.

HIKING SPOTS

This region retains a great deal of unspoiled natural beauty. On Capri, one of the best hikes is up the Scala Fenicia to Anacapri and then on up to the top, Monte Solaro. On Ischia, head up Via Monterone or Via Bocca from Forio, through the Falanga Forest to the summit of Monte Epomeo. Along the Amalfi Coast, walk the Sentiero degli Dei, from Montepertuso.

7 Sorrento
D5

Palisades and grand hotels notwithstanding, there is no getting around the fact that Sorrento can be chaotic. Yet the town has been a resort since the 1700s – Casanova and Goethe are two notable past visitors – and there is certainly plenty of charm to be found in the old streets.

8 Capri
The fabled isle *(p42)* has had its detractors – it has been called "nothing more than a rocky cliff with over-priced cafés" – and, in ancient times, the notorious shenanigans of Tiberius gave it an enduring reputation as a decadent spot, as did the party life here in the 1950s. Yet, if you choose to stay awhile, you will discover the real Capri beyond the hype – a world of traditional farm life, scenic hiking terrain and sparkling azure waters for swimming and boating.

9 Massa Lubrense
D5

To the west of Sorrento, this is one of several fishing villages clustered around little ports. Rarely crowded, the site affords wonderful views across to Capri from the belvedere in Largo Vescovado. At Marina della Lobra there's a beach.

10 Nerano
D5

While administratively part of Massa Lubrense on the northern side of the peninsula, the remote location of this quiet fishing village on the southern side means fine views and a scenic beach in the seaside hamlet of Marina del Cantone. It has an atmospheric setting, sophisticated seaside dining, and fine hiking along the rugged coastline, including the protected nature reserve at Punta Campanella.

**Ravello on the serene
Amalfi Coast**

A DAY'S ISLAND HOPPING

Morning

The tour begins on the island of **Procida**. Either take the first hydrofoil from Naples-Beverello (40 min) or the first ferry from Pozzuoli (30 min) to get here. You will arrive at Marina Grande, greeted by the sight of fishing boats and the colourful houses lining the port. Take a quick hike to the island's highest point, the **Terra Murata** ("Walled Town").

Back down on the marina, enjoy some refreshment at **Bar Capriccio** on Via Roma 99 while waiting for your hydrofoil to **Ischia** *(p104)*.

Your boat to Ischia will arrive at **Casamicciola**, the island's second port, where you can have lunch at the **Il Focolare** on Via Cretajo al Crocefisso 3.

Afternoon

Take a tour around the island in a boat, stopping by at the town of **Sant'Angelo**. Lounge by the dockside or walk along the cliff above **Maronti Beach**.

You can stay in one of the hotels in Casamicciola, or take a hydrofoil back to the mainland. If you spend the night, take the hydrofoil or one of the ferries to **Capri** *(p42)* the next morning. After riding the funicular up to Capri Town, follow the signs up to the ruins of Villa Jovis for the breathtaking views.

Picturesque village of Atrani on the Amalfi Coast

Amalfi Coast Sights

1. Positano
📍 E5 🏛 Via Regina Giovanna 13
🌐 aziendaturismopositano.it

A vertical town in shades of pink and faded pastels, known for decades as a playground for the rich and famous. Only one street winds through the village with steps leading down to the beach and the heart of the village.

2. Scala
📍 E4

Across the valley from Ravello, Scala offers the best view of Ravello and is also the starting point for hikes to Amalfi and the Valle delle Ferriere.

3. Praiano
📍 E5

With incredible views of the ocean, this little village on a clifftop is home to Marina di Praia, a pretty pebble beach.

4. Amalfi
📍 E5 🏛 Corso delle Repubbliche Marinare 11 🌐 amalfitouristoffice.it

The largest and most historic town on its coastline. The architecture evokes its former mercantile glory . The 9th-century *Duomo* (cathedral), is a must-see.

5. Atrani
📍 E5 🏛 San Salvatore de' Birecto, Piazzetta Umberto I

This little town exudes a quiet charm, with its arcades and a maze of alley-stairways. Amalfi's doges were invested at its church, San Salvatore de' Birecto.

6. Ravello
📍 E5 🏛 Piazza Fontana Moresca 10
📞 089 85 70 96

In the 13th century, Ravello was an important player in the sea trade. Its medieval look accounts for its beauty.

7. Minori and Maiori
📍 E5–F5

Maiori has the coast's longest beach, while Minori is home to the archaeological site, the Villa Romana.

8. Cetara
📍 F4

Home to the coast's most active fishing fleet, it sells *colatura di alici*, a fish sauce descended from the ancient Roman *garum*. A fishing boat festival takes place every year in early August.

9. Vietri sul Mare
📍 F4

Vietri is famous for its ceramics, which originated in the 1400s and are still handcrafted and hand-painted.

10. Conca dei Marini
📍 E5

This town is known for the luminous light at the *Grotta dello Smeraldo* (Emerald Grotto), which can only be visited by boat. Other attractions include the town's pretty marina and a 16th-century watchtower. The views from the ocean-facing San Pancrazio Church are stunning, making it a popular spot for weddings.

Museums

1. Certosa di San Giacomo, Capri
⊙ U2 ⌂ Via Certosa 10 ☎ 081 837 62 18 ⊙ 10am–5:30pm Tue–Sun
This 14th-century monastery features North African-style vaults forming little domes.

2. Arsenale Museum, Amalfi
⊙ E5 ⌂ Largo Cesario Console 3 ⊙ Hours vary, check website ⊛ arsenalediamalfi.it
This museum traces the history of the Republic of Amalfi and its contributions to the development of the compass and maritime laws.

3. Villa San Michele, Anacapri
⊙ S1 ⌂ Viale Axel Munthe 34 ⊙ Hours vary, check website ⊛ villasanmichele.eu ⌷
Marbles and furnishings from the 17th to 19th centuries are found in this villa.

4. Castello Aragonese, Ischia
⊙ B4 ⌂ Ischia Ponte ⊙ 9am–sunset daily ⊛ castelloaragonese ischia.com ⌷
In the 16th century poetess Vittoria Colonna held court here, making Ischia the cultural centre of the Mediterranean.

5. Villa Romana, Minori
⊙ E5 ⌂ Via Capo Di Piazza 28 ☎ 089 85 28 93 ⊙ 9am–7pm Tue–Sat, 8am–1:30pm Sun
In this villa the fresco style dates from the 1st century CE. Excavated artifacts are also displayed here.

6. Abbazia di San Michele Arcangelo, Procida
⊙ B4 ⌂ Terra Murata ☎ 081 896 76 12 ⊙ 10am–12:45pm daily; also 4–6:30pm Tue–Fri ⌷
This 11th-century abbey, dominating the majestic walled citadel on Terra Murata, is known for paintings by pupils of Luca Giordano.

7. Antiquarium Silio Italico
⊙ D4 ⌂ Casa Municipale, Via Filangieri 98 ☎ 081 801 92 42 ⊙ 9am–2pm Mon–Fri
Archaeological finds from this Roman town consist of pottery, decorative figurines and tools.

8. Museo Correale di Terranova, Sorrento
⊙ D5 ⌂ Via Correale 50 ⊙ 9am–6pm Tue–Sat, 9am–1pm Sun & hols ⊛ museocorreale.it ⌷
Housed in an ancient villa, this 18th-century villa is one of Sorrento's most important museums. It houses archaeological finds including a 4th-century BCE Greek original of Artemis on a Deer.

9. Museo Archeologico Georges Vallet, Piano di Sorrento
⊙ D5 ⌂ Via Ripa di Cassano ☎ 081 808 70 78 ⊙ 9am–1pm Tue, Thu & Sat, 12:30–5:30pm Tue, Fri & Sun
This museum displays finds from all over the peninsula, including pottery and weapons.

10. Casa Rossa, Anacapri
⊙ T1 ⌂ Via G. Orlandi 78 ☎ 081 838 2193 ⊙ 10am–1:30pm & 4:30–8pm Tue–Sun ⌷
Located on a long lane that is home to artisanal workshops, Casa Rossa features local art and is notable for Roman statues from the Blue Grotto.

Roman statue at Casa Rossa in Anacapri

Shopping

1. Canfora, Capri
🅥 U1 🅐 Via Camerelle 3
🅦 canfora.com
Cobblers friendlier than these would be hard to find. Stop by to pick out designs you like and within a few hours – unless you choose something extra fancy – you'll have your hand-tooled, custom-made sandals.

2. Corallium, Anacapri
🅥 T1 🅐 Via G Orlandi 50
A coral and cameo factory in Anacapri. The selection is extraordinary, created with both silver and gold, and prices are excellent. A certificate of guarantee comes with every purchase.

3. Salvatore Gargiulo, Sorrento
🅥 D5 🅐 Via Fuoro 33
Examples of Sorrentine intarsia (marquetry) are to be seen all over town, but this workshop turns out top-quality products at reasonable prices. Note the music boxes.

4. Carthusia, Capri
🅥 U2 🅐 Via Camerelle 10
The closest you can come to bringing the natural beauty of Capri home is with Carthusia's collection of perfumes inspired by and created on Capri. Fragrances, soaps and home scents make beautiful gifts.

5. Limonoro, Sorrento
🅥 D5 🅐 Via S Cesareo 49
One of the top souvenirs from the area is limoncello, the signature lemon liqueur. This is a good place to watch it being made, after which you'll understand why it packs such a punch – it's basically pure alcohol with flavourings.

6. Tavassi, Capri
🅥 T1 🅐 Via G Orlandi 129
Some of the best ceramics on the island. Designs tend to evoke the natural hues of the setting – azure, gold, green – usually with flowers and vines or other florid vegetation. Anything can be designed to your specifications and you can watch the artists at work.

7. La Scuderia del Duca, Amalfi
🅥 E5 🅐 Largo Cesareo Console 8
Amalfi's handmade paper-making tradition is vibrantly on display in this beautiful shop.

8. Camo, Ravello
🅥 E4 🅐 Piazza Duomo 9
A factory (and museum) that sells cameos and beautiful coral jewellery.

9. Ceramiche d'Arte Carmela, Ravello
🅥 E4 🅐 Via dei Rufolo 16
This workshop is the place to come for gorgeous ceramics decorated with traditional designs.

10. Milleunaceramica, Amalfi
🅥 E5 🅐 Via Pietro Capuano 36
A treasure trove of locally produced ceramics, this shop offers items that are handpicked by the owner and created by artisans.

Perfumes and fragrances on offer at Carthusia

Bustling La Piazzetta in Capri's old town

Nightlife

1. La Piazzetta, Capri
U1
Capri Town's main square may be small but it's big on *la vita mondana* (sophisticated lifestyle). The little bars, with their cluster of outdoor tables, are a magnet for daytrippers and locals alike, although the latter generally turn up after dark when the former have moved on.

2. Capri Rooftop, Capri
U2 **Via Matteotti 7**
There's no better place to gather with friends for drinks than on this sophisticated lounge's sweeping terrace, overlooking the Faraglioni rock stacks.

3. Qubè Cafè, Capri
U1 **Via li Curti 6**
A quirky disco-bar a short stroll from Capri's stylish Piazzetta. With a local feel that's a refreshing change from the island's posh night spots, music varies from classic rock to electronic.

4. Discoteca Valentino Pianobar, Ischia
B4 **Corso Vittoria Colonna 97**
This old-school club still attracts a young, energetic crowd.

5. Chaplin's Pub, Sorrento
D5 **Corso Italia 18**
A delightful mix of Irish and Italian, this friendly, family-owned Irish pub in the heart of Sorrento offers an excellent beer selection.

6. Music on the Rocks, Positano
E5 **Grotta dell'Incanto 51**
Set inside a cavern, this beachside disco pub is the hot spot for nightlife on the Amalfi Coast. At weekends it is a high-energy nightclub featuring international DJs and live music. Cover charge.

7. Taverna Anema e Core, Capri
U1 **Via Sella Orta 1**
Oct–Mar: Mon–Fri
The "Soul and Heart" taverna is still redolent of la dolce vita vibes of decades past and is considered Capri's premier nightclub. It attracts a chic, yet fun-loving crowd.

8. Annunziata Church, Ravello
E4 **Via della Annunziata**
Dating from the Middle Ages, this church is no longer used for religious services; bar the Ravello Concert Society presents year-round chamber concerts in this evocative setting.

9. VV Club Capri
U1 **Via Vittorio Emanuele 45**
Midnight–5:30am Sat
Buzzing club with resident and international guest DJs on the decks, special Latin music nights and tasty cocktails.

10. Villa Rufolo, Ravello
E4 **Piazza Duomo** **9am–7pm daily** **villarufolo.com**
Jazz concerts and classical recitals are held in the grounds of the Villa Rufolo from June to September.

Pizzerie, Cafés and Gelaterie

Patrons enjoying a meal at La Zagara, Positano

1. La Zagara, Positano
 E5 Via dei Mulini 10 · €€

La Zagara is a major tourist magnet, but there's no denying that the treats they serve here are delicious: pastries, cakes, fresh fruit sorbets and the like. The patio, with fragrant lemon trees, is captivating.

2. Gran Caffè, Amalfi
 E5 Corso delle Repubbliche Marinare 37/38 · €

With picturesque outdoor seating overlooking the beach and port of Amalfi, this café is a popular spot with locals and visitors for enjoying drinks or a light meal. The sunset views are spectacular.

3. Bar Tiberio, Capri
 U1 La Piazzetta · €€

One of the main bars on the Piazzetta, but everyone has his or her own favourite. Great for people-watching.

4. Bar Calise, Ischia
 B4 Via Antonio Sogliuzzo 69 · €

One of the island's best bars, with excellent gelato (ice cream) and *dolci* (desserts). It's surrounded by dense greenery in the middle of a traffic circle in this laid-back port.

5. Da Maria, Amalfi
 E5 Via Lorenzo d'Amalfi 14
 089 87 18 80 Mon · €€

Amalfi's best wood-fired pizza can be found at this friendly place near Piazza Duomo. Local specialities also feature on the menu.

6. Villa Verde, Capri
 U1 Vico Sella Orta 6
 081 837 70 24 · €€€

Offering spacious indoor seating as well as a lush garden, this restaurant has exquisite focaccia and pizza and an excellent house red from Calabria.

7. Pasticceria Pansa, Amalfi
 E5 Piazza Duomo 40 · €

An Amalfi institution since 1830, this elegant bar offers a wide selection of sweets and locally made chocolates. The chocolate covered citrus peels are a treat. Outdoor tables provide a good view of the main square.

8. Da Pasquale, Sant'Angelo, Ischia
 B4 Via Sant'Angelo 79
 081 90 42 08 · €

Dining is home-style here, even to the occasional sharing of tables and bench seating. The pizza is tasty and there's a good choice of beer and wine.

9. Sant'Antonino, Sorrento
 D5 Via Santa Maria delle Grazie 6
 081 877 12 00 · €€

Excellent, wood-fired pizza is served here for lunch and dinner. The heat of traditional wood ovens flash-bakes the dough, preventing the toppings from becoming soggy.

10. Nonna Sceppa, Paestum
 H6 Via Laura 45 082 885 10 64
 Thu · €€€

The least touristy of the choices here is a highly recommended restaurant that has excellent pizzas, seafood and delicious home-style dishes.

Restaurants

1. La Cambusa, Positano
⊙ E5 **⌂** Piazza A Vespucci 4
☎ 089 87 54 32 · €€
Positioned to the right of the beach, with dining on a porticoed balcony. Seafood is the thing to go for.

2. Terrazza Bosquet, Sorrento
⊙ D5 **⌂** Grand Hotel Excelsior Vittoria, Piazza Tasso 34 **☎** 081 877 71 11 · €€€
The grandest experience Sorrento offers, in the frescoed dining room of this superlative hotel. Silver, china, crystal and fine linen complement the service.

3. Villa Maria, Ravello
⊙ E4 **⌂** Via Santa Chiari 2
☎ 089 85 72 55 · €€€
With a pergola-covered dining terrace and a breathtaking setting this is a peaceful respite for savouring the views and Ravello specialities.

4. Buca di Bacco "da Serafina", Capri
⊙ U1 **⌂** Via Longano 35 **☎** 081 837 07 23 **⊘** Mon · €€
This place is top of most locals' list, for both quality and price. Cooking features seafood, *antipasti* and pizza.

5. Marina Grande, Amalfi
⊙ E5 **⌂** Via della Regione 4
☎ 089 87 11 29 · €€
One of the best restaurants in town, right on the sea. Dishes include seafood ravioli with arugula (rocket) sauce.

6. Da Paolino Lemon Trees, Capri
⊙ T1 **⌂** Via Palazzo e Mare 11
☎ 081 837 61 02 · €€€
Enjoy romantic outdoor dining under the lemon trees at this country-style restaurant known for its traditional Caprese dishes.

7. Il Solitario, Anacapri
⊙ T1 **⌂** Via G Orlandi 96
☎ 081 837 13 82 · €€
This delightful place serves homemade food with the freshest ingredients the season has to offer.

8. La Conchiglia, Chiaia Beach, Procida
⊙ B4 **⌂** Steps from Via Pizzaco 10
☎ 081 896 76 02 **⊘** Nov–Mar · €€
Arrive at this spot by walking down 183 steps from Piazza Olmo or reserve a boat trip from Corricella. Try the pasta with sweet mussels and courgette.

9. Alberto al Mare, Ischia
⊙ B4 **⌂** Lungomare Cristoforo Colombo 8 **☎** 081 98 12 59 · €€€
Located over the water, the bounty of the sea is the speciality here. Options might include swordfish or monkfish.

10. Don Alfonso 1890, Sorrentine Peninsula
⊙ D5 **⌂** Sant'Agata sui Due Golfi, Corso Sant' Agata 13 **☎** 081 878 00 26 **⊘** Mon & Wed; Dec & Mar · €€€
With two Michelin stars expect impeccable food. The tasting menus and wines are superb.

Dining on the pier at Marina Grande, Amalfi

POSILLIPO, POZZUOLI AND THE NORTH

If central seaside Naples is known as "Royal Naples", the coastal area to the west could be called "Imperial Naples" for its enormous popularity with imperial families and their courtiers in ancient Roman times. Significant ruins left by them are everywhere, hiding behind the post-war *abusivo* (illegal) building developments that now blot the landscape. However, the area is subject to one of nature's stranger phenomena. Bradyseism is underground volcanic activity that gives rise to "slow earthquakes", resulting in the continual rising and lowering of the land, and making it an unstable base for settlement. The region is relatively unexplored by modern-day tourists but was top of the list for those who took the 19th-century Grand Tour, not least because it has one of Italy's finest palaces, the Reggia di Caserta.

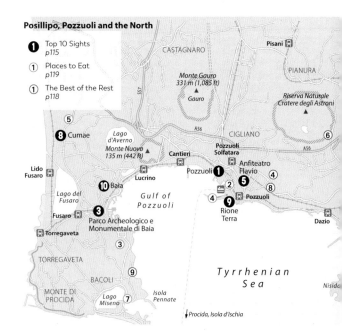

Posillipo, Pozzuoli and the North

1 Top 10 Sights
p115

1 Places to Eat
p119

1 The Best of the Rest
p118

Fishing boats moored at the quaint town of Marechiaro

1 Pozzuoli
C3

Called Puteoli by the Romans, this seaside town was a major player 2,000 years ago. Its ruins include the archaeological site of Rione Terra and the Serapeum, thought for centuries to be a temple of the Egyptian god Serapis but now known to be a market. Puteoli was the main imperial port and retained its importance even after the Port of Ostia was upgraded by Emperor Trajan in the 2nd century.

2 Marechiaro

One of the most romantic spots on this evocative coastline, this little fishing village offers great views from Via Marechiaro. The panoramic vista of Vesuvius from here is repeatedly celebrated, most nostalgically in the quintessential song 'O Sole Mio by Neapolitan artist Salvatore di Giacomo. Further down, the village is lined with bars, cafés and restaurants overlooking the water.

3 Parco Archeologico e Monumentale di Baia
B3 **Via Castello** **9am–2pm Tue–Sun** **cultura.gov.it**

Arranged in terraces, this excavated area features an ancient spa and a Temple of Diana. The spa complex comprises baths named after Venus and Mercury, with the latter being a particularly large swimming pool once covered with a dome.

4 Capo di Posillipo
J2

The ancient Greeks called the area Pausilypon ("respite from pain") due to the great beauty of the place. Through the ages, it retained its appeal due to a succession of inhabitants and visitors, from religious communities in medieval times to holiday resorts for the Spanish aristocracy in the 17th century. However, the area was heavily overbuilt following World War II with the unregulated spread of ugly apartment buildings. Fortunately, parts of the area down by the water still retain great charm.

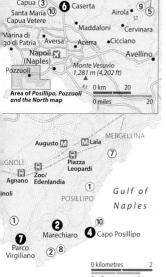

Ruins of the ancient Roman
Anfiteatro Flavio

5 Anfiteatro Flavio

📍 C3 📌 Corso Terracciano
75, Pozzuoli 📞 081 526 60 07 🕐 9am–
1 hour before sunset Wed–Mon 🔗

This is the third-largest Roman
amphitheatre in the world, after
those at Rome and Capua. It seated
40,000 and had an array of below-floor
apparatus for making the *venationes*
(wild animal "hunts") that took place
as theatrical as possible.

6 Reggia di Caserta

📍 D1 📌 Viale Douhet 2/a
🕐 Hours vary, chech website
🌐 reggiadicaserta.cultura.gov.it 🔗

Neapolitan Baroque at its most refined,
this 18th-century palace is set around
four courtyards with lavish rooms,
highlighted by the Great Staircase
and the Throne Room. The park has

Exquisite carved staircases at
the Reggia di Caserta

huge decorated fountains, culminating
in the Grande Cascata.

7 Parco Virgiliano

📍 J2 📌 Viale Virgilio 🕐 May & Jun:
7am–midnight, Jul–Sep: 7am–1am,
Oct–Apr: 7am–9pm 🔗

Occupying the summit of a hill, this
park has amazing views. Below lies
the island of Nisida, formed from an
ancient volcanic crater and connected
by a causeway.

8 Cumae

📍 B3 📌 Via Monte di Cuma 1
📞 081 854 30 60 🕐 9am–1 hour before
sunset Wed–Mon 🔗

Founded in the 8th century BCE,
Cumae played a big part in history,

THE BURNING FIELDS

Flegrei and Phlegrean derive from
a Greek word *phlegraios* (burning),
applied in ancient times to this zone
of perpetual, low-level volcanic
activity. Beneath the earth's surface
here, magma (molten rock) is flowing,
applying pressure upward, making
it one of the most unstable regions
of the earth's crust, literally littered
with volcanic cones and craters.

Trapezoidal entrance to Sibyl's Grotto in Cumae

due to its seeress. The Cumaean Sibyl, priestess of Apollo, was an oracle who exerted great influence, and leaders of Rome depended on her prophecies. She also appeared in Virgil's *Aeneid*. Sibyl's Grotto *(p67)*, with its trapezoidal entrance tunnel, is an enigmatic experience.

9 Rione Terra

C3 ⬢ Largo Sedile di Porta ☎ 063 996 71 25 ⬤ 9am–5:30pm daily ⬢

This excavation site continues to reveal the remains of a Roman settlement underneath the abandoned Spanish town on the hilltop. After exploring the Roman streets, you'll emerge at the baroque Cathedral of San Procolo, supported by the giant columns of the long-hidden Temple of Augustus. It is advisable to book your visit in advance.

10 Baia

B3

Originally, this town was one of the most sumptuous resorts of the ancient world. Due to seismic activity in this area, it is now a flooded city *(p51)* that can be explored by dives or by boat. There's also a 15th-century castle, the Castello di Baia *(081 523 37 97)*, housing an archaeological museum, while to the north is Lago d'Averno, a crater lake that the ancients believed marked the entrance to the Underworld. To the east of town is the Villa Volpicelli, appearing like a floating castle along the edge of Lago del Fusaro.

A MORNING IN ANCIENT POZZUOLI

Begin your tour in the morning with a visit to **Solfatara** *(p118)*, the vast volcanic lava cap about 1 km (0.5 mile) north of the town. While Solfatara is currently closed, the crater can still be seen by heading up Via Solfatara. Next, head back to town on the **Via Vecchia di San Gennaro** and turn left onto Via Domiziana, following the ancient Roman road of basalt stones built to link Rome to Puteoli (Pozzuoli; *p115*). Visit the **Santuario di San Gennaro** *(p118)* and see the spot where Naples' patron saint met his martyrdom under Emperor Diocletian.

Descend Via Vecchia di San Gennaro to Piscina Cardito, a 2nd-century cistern with a vaulted ceiling supported by pillars. Continue to the **Anfiteatro Flavio** and explore its ruins. Follow Via Terracciano to the Terme dette Tempio di Nettuno's huge terraced baths. On the opposite slope is the Ninfeo di Diana, a fountain that may have been part of the baths.

Work your way down towards the ancient port, now mostly submerged, to the Serapeum (market). Then walk up onto the promontory, **Rione Terra** to explore the 2,000-year-old **Duomo** (cathedral).

Finally, enjoy lunch at **Antica Trattoria da Ciuffiello** *(p119)*.

The Best of the Rest

1. Science City, Bagnoli
📍 J2 🏠 Via Coroglio 104 🕐 9am–5pm Tue–Sun 🌐 cittadellascienza.it ♿

This science centre is designed to educate and amuse kids of all ages. Book in advance to avoid long queues.

2. Santa Maria del Faro, Posillipo
📍 J2 🏠 Via Marechiaro 96a
📞 081 769 14 39 🕐 For mass

Dating back to the 1300s, this church was probably built over the remains of a Roman *faro* (lighthouse).

3. Museo Provinciale Campano di Capua
📍 C1 🏠 Via Roma 68 🕐 9am–5:30pm Tue–Fri, 9am–1:30pm Sat & 9am–1pm Sun 🌐 museocampanocapua.it ♿

The wealth of ancient Capua is on display in this museum.

4. Solfatara, Pozzuoli
📍 C3 🏠 Via Solfatara 161
🕐 8:30am–1 hour before sunset daily 🌐 solfatara.it ♿

Above the town, this crater of a dormant volcano has an unearthly landscape.

5. Benevento
📍 F1

This town's pride and joy is the well-preserved Arch of Trajan, chronicling the Roman emperor's civic works.

Ancient Roman Arch of Trajan in Benevento

6. Cratere degli Astroni
📍 C3 🏠 Via Agnano Agli Astroni 468 🕐 Hours vary, chech website 🌐 crateredegliastroni.org ♿

The Romans tapped the geothermal properties of this volcanic crater to build their spas.

7. Palazzo Donn'Anna, Posillipo
📍 J2 🏠 Piazza Donn'Anna 9
🚫 To the public

Rumour has it that Queen Joan II used this 17th-century palace for illicit trysts after which she had her lovers tossed into the sea.

8. Santuario di San Gennaro, Pozzuoli
📍 C3 🏠 Via S Gennaro Agnano 8
📞 081 526 11 14 🕐 7:30–11am & 4–6:45pm Mon–Sat, 7:30am–1:15pm & 4:30–6:45pm Sun

This 16th-century church is said to mark the spot where Naples' patron saint was decapitated.

9. Piscina Mirabilis: Bacoli
📍 B4 🏠 Via Piscina Mirabile 27
🕐 10am–4pm Fri–Sun ♿

Noteworthy here is the Piscina Mirabilis, a cistern used to collect water for the old port of Misenum.

10. Santa Maria Capua Vetere
📍 C1

Today, Capua is home to a ruined amphitheatre and an ancient temple.

Places to Eat

Pasta paccheri with prawns at Don Antonio 2.0

1. Gelateria Bilancione, Posillipo
◻ J2 ◻ Via Posillipo 238 ◻ gelateria bilancioneposillipo.it · €
Take in the vista while enjoying your favourite *gelato* at this ice cream shop.

2. Antica Trattoria da Ciuffiello, Pozzuoli
◻ C3 ◻ Via Dicearchia 11 bis ◻ 081 526 93 97 ◻ Mon · €€
Known for its grilled specialities, this restaurant offers *zuppa di pesce* (fish soup), which is a meal in itself.

3. A Casa di Tobia, Bacoli
◻ B4 ◻ Via Fondi di Baia 12 ◻ 081 523 51 93 ◻ Mon & D Sun · €€
Wonderful organically grown food, from the rich volcanic soil of the crater on which the place is perched. It is best to book ahead.

4. Don Antonio 2.0, Pozzuoli
◻ C3 ◻ Vico Magazzini 20 ◻ 081 048 60 18 ◻ Mon · €€
Among the best seafood restaurants lining Pozzuoli's harbour. Don Antonio 2.0 offers excellent and reasonably priced fish pasta dishes.

5. Vinaria, Pozzuoli
◻ C3 ◻ Via Monte di Cuma 3 ◻ 081 804 62 35 ◻ Mon–Thu & D Sun · €€€
This restaurant enjoys its own piece of history with Roman ruins discovered on site. The wine list highlights bottles from Campania and Campi Flegrei.

6. Da Teresa, Casertavecchia
◻ D1 ◻ Via Torre 4 ◻ 329 364 30 41 ◻ Wed · €€
Da Teresa offers great views over Caserta and serves generously portioned set meals of mountain game or seafood.

7. Da Fefè, Bacoli
◻ B4 ◻ Via della Shoah 15, Casevecchie ◻ fefeabacoli.it · €€
Filled with regulars, this place faces the port. You are welcomed with the house aperitif and advised of the seafood specials of the day.

8. 'A Fenestella, Marechiaro
◻ J2 ◻ Via Marechiaro 23 ◻ Tue ◻ ristoranteafenestella.it · €€€
Along with typical Neapolitan dishes, this restaurant offers the best seafood. You can take in views of Marechiaro's picturesque harbour. Save room for the delicious *babà*!

9. Da Gino e Pina, Benevento
◻ F1 ◻ Viale dell' Università 23 ◻ 082 42 49 47 ◻ L Sat, D Sun; Aug · €€
A popular family-run restaurant serving traditional cuisine using local produce. Try the homemade pasta in local saffron liqueur. It has a great selection of homemade desserts.

10. Riva Restaurant, Posillipo
◻ J2 ◻ Via Russo 13 ◻ 081 769 12 78 ◻ L Mon–Fri · €€€
Dine in style and enjoy the flavours of the sun-soaked Italian coast at this restaurant. The seafood is excellent. It is a popular venue for receptions and celebrations, so book ahead.

STREETSMART

A fresh Neapolitan pizza

GETTING AROUND

Whether you are visiting for a weekend city break or a long and luxurious coastal retreat, here is everything you need to know about navigating Naples and the Amalfi Coast.

AT A GLANCE

PUBLIC TRANSPORT COSTS

NAPLES METRO

€1.10

Single metro journey

NAPLES TO SORRENTO

€4.10

Single journey on Circumvesuviana

AMALFI COAST

€10.00

24 hours unlimited on Costierasita buses

TOP TIP
Save time and hassle by downloading the Unico Campania transport app.

SPEED LIMIT

MOTORWAY	DUAL CARRIAGEWAY
130 km/h (80 mph)	**110** km/h (68 mph)

SECONDARY ROAD	URBAN AREA
90 km/h (56 mph)	**50** km/h (30 mph)

Arriving by Air

Naples International Airport is the main airport for flights to Naples, the Amalfi Coast and the general Campania region. Non-stop services from major hubs like London and New York are available, while many more airlines offer a layover in Rome first. European budget airlines fly to Naples at very reasonable prices. The airport is easy to navigate, although it gets busy in the summer months with the inflow of high-season travellers. For outbound travellers, there are plenty of shopping and dining facilities once through security at the terminal.
Naples International Airport
W aeroportodinapoli.it/en

International Train Travel

Regular high-speed international trains (both direct and with changes) link Naples to several towns and cities across Europe. These include London, Paris, Nice, Berlin, Munich, Amsterdam, Vienna, Lisbon, Geneva, Brussels, Barcelona, Budapest, Warsaw and Ljubljana. **Eurail** and **Interrail** sell passes (to European non-residents and residents respectively) for international trips lasting from five days up to three months. Journeys should be reserved in advance.
Eurail
W eurail.com
Interrail
W interrail.eu

Domestic Train Travel

Naples is also well connected to other main towns and cities within Italy. Both **Trenitalia**, the main train operator within Italy, and **Italo Treno** (NTV) offer a high-speed service between major railway stations throughout the country. Making reservations for these services is essential and tickets are booked up quickly, so try to buy as far ahead as possible. Trips usually require a change in Rome, which is under 90 minutes away by high-speed train from the main railway station in Naples, **Napoli Centrale**.

Operated by **Ente Autonomo Volturno** (EAV), the Circumvesuviana links Naples to Sorrento (1hr 10min; €4.10) and its many stops include Herculaneum and Pompeii. In the summer months, the comfortable Campania Express runs the same route in just 30 minutes for €8.

Ente Autonomo Volturno
W eavsrl.it
Italo Treno
W italotreno.it
Napoli Centrale
W napolicentrale.it
Trenitalia
W trenitalia.com

Public Transport
ANM is Naples' main public transport authority. Safety and hygiene measures, timetables, ticket information and transport maps can be obtained from ANM's website or app, Gira Napoli.
ANM
W anm.it

Tickets
Unico Campania offers 1-day or weekly tickets for integrated travel on metro, funicular, bus and train services in Naples and regions in Campania. Single tickets for Naples Metro cost €1.10 from ticket windows or machines, 90-minute tickets for all Naples public transport cost €1.60, and day passes cost €4.50. Tickets are validated upon being inserted at the turnstile. Use the ticket to exit the station. European card-holders can purchase tickets with the Unico Campania app.
Unico Campania
W unicocampania.it

Long-Distance Buses
The **SITA** bus service connects towns on the Amalfi Coast between Sorrento and Salerno. The Costierasita day pass costs €10, affording unlimited bus travel in this region for 24 hours from ticket validation. Tickets generally need to be purchased at a local tobacconist (tabacchi) before boarding and seats cannot be reserved. Those suffering from motion sickness should be prepared for a twisting ride through the hills of the Amalfi Coast.

Capri, **Ischia** and **Procida** all have local bus services around the islands. Be sure to check the schedules.
Capri
W capri.com/en/getting-around
Ischia
W ischia.it
Procida
W visitprocida.com
SITA
W sitasudtrasporti.it

TRAVEL BETWEEN KEY DESTINATIONS

From	To	Distance	Transport	Time	Price
Naples airport	Railway station	5 km (3 miles)	Alibus	20 mins	€5
Naples airport	Railway station	5 km (3 miles)	Taxi	15 mins	from €15
Naples	Sorrento	47 km (29 miles)	Train	30-75 mins	€4–8
Naples	Sorrento	47 km (29 miles)	Ferry	35-55 mins	from €15
Naples	Capri	45 km (28 miles)	Ferry	45-50 mins	from €23
Naples	Procida	35 km (22 miles)	Ferry	30-40 mins	from €9
Naples	Ischia	56 km (35 miles)	Ferry	50-90 mins	from €13
Sorrento	Positano	16 km (10 miles)	SITA bus	50 mins	€2.60
Sorrento	Praiano	23 km (14 miles)	SITA bus	70 mins	€3.20
Sorrento	Amalfi	31 km (19 miles)	SITA bus	110 mins	€4
Sorrento	Ravello	38 km (24 miles)	SITA bus	120 mins	€4
Sorrento	Salerno	56 km (35 miles)	SITA bus	120 mins	€4.60

Metro, Funiculars and Buses

Naples Metro has a fairly straight-forward system with Linea 1, Linea 2, Linea 6 and the Napoli-Aversa line. Art fans may want to explore Linea 1, known as the Metro dell'Arte for the contemporary works of art that have been installed in many of its stations.

More important for visitors are the many funiculars that transport people up and down the hills in Naples – a welcome alternative to walking up steep staircases. Naples has four funiculars, linking the centre to Vomero and Posillipo. Capri Town has one.

Until the metro's Linea 1 opens its Aeroporto station (scheduled for 2026), buses are the best way to get to the airport, around the Amalfi Coast and around the islands. Due to traffic congestion within the city of Naples, however, they are not always the fastest way to get around the centre. The **Hop On Hop Off** buses are a good option for an overview of the city's main sights.

Hop On Hop Off
W hop-on-hop-off-bus.com
Naples Metro
W anm.it

Taxis

Naples has a reputation for taxi scams, but it is an easy thing to avoid. Licensed taxis have a menu of fares posted in the car that you can ask to see, and fares are determined based on the starting point and destination as marked on it. While most drivers are honest, tourists may sometimes be charged double unless the fare was clearly defined before the trip. If a driver tries to suggest that it is a holiday or that the fares do not apply, do not board the taxi. Avoid drivers who seem too eager to pick you up. Visit **Napoli Unplugged** for useful taxi information. Private services like Uber are not available.

Napoli Unplugged
W napoliunplugged.com/naples-taxi-services

Driving

One of the best ways to explore Italy is by car. However, it can also be a hair-raising experience for those unfamiliar with Italian driving culture. Make sure you are familiar with the rules of the road and have all the necessary documentation, as traffic police (carabinieri) carry out checks.

Car Rental

To rent a car in Italy you must be over 21 and have held a valid driver's licence for at least a year. Some companies may allow drivers to rent at the age of 18 if they have held their licence for at least one year. Most apply young driver surcharges for under 25s. Driving licences issued by any of the EU member states are valid in Italy. If visiting from outside the EU, you may need to apply for an International Driving Permit (IDP). Most rental agencies in Naples operate near the main train station, allowing drivers to avoid the traffic of the central areas.

Driving to Naples

While driving within Naples is challenging, a car can be an easy way to get to and around the region. If you bring your own foreign-registered car into the country, you must carry a Green Card, the vehicle's registration documents and a valid driver's licence with you when driving. Main towns and cities often enforce a ZTL (Limited Traffic Zone). To avoid fines, consult the **Urban Access Regulations in Europe**.

Toll fees are payable on most motorways (autostrade), and payment is made at the end of the journey by cash, credit card or pre-paid magnetic VIA cards – available from manned toll gates, tobacconists and the **ACI** (Automobile Club d'Italia). Alternatively, make use of the "Telepass" lanes by buying a Telepass at www.tolltickets.com. You can also avoid tolls altogether by using the national roads (strade nazionali) or secondary state roads (strade statali).

Although less direct, they are often more scenic. One of the most famous, the Amalfi Drive (State Road 163), connects Amalfi Coast towns along a winding route.

ACI
w aci.it
Urban Access Regulations in Europe
w urbanaccessregulations.eu

Rules of the Road
Drive on the right, use the left lane only for passing, and yield to traffic from the right. Seat belts are required for all passengers in the front and back, and heavy fines are levied for using a mobile phone while driving. Dipped headlights are compulsory during the day on motorways, dual carriageways and on all out-of-town roads.

A red warning triangle, fluorescent vests and spare tyre must be carried at all times for use in an emergency. If you have an accident or breakdown, switch on your hazard warning lights and place the triangle approximately 50 m (55 yd) behind your vehicle. For breakdowns call the ACI (116) or the emergency services (112 or 113). The ACI will tow any foreign-registered vehicle to the nearest affiliated garage free of charge.

Bicycle and Scooter Hire
It is not advisable to try riding motorbikes or scooters in Naples unless you have a good deal of prior experience. Bicycles are not a common sight in the city, and cycling is generally discouraged. Traffic is difficult to navigate and cobbled streets make it harder and less enjoyable than simply walking or taking public transport. However, all three are much more viable options on the islands and along the Amalfi Coast, where e-bikes in particular are increasingly popular. Note that the region is incredibly hilly, and though drivers have become increasingly accustomed to seeing cyclists on the roads, reckless driving is unfortunately still common.

Cycling has become popular around the coast and on the islands, but there aren't a good deal of bicycle hire shops. Your best bet is to enquire at your hotel about the nearest option.

Walking
Walking is a great way to explore Naples and other towns, but always pay close attention to traffic. On the Amalfi Coast and the islands, cross-country walks can be a peaceful adventure for those who are reasonably fit. The famed Sentiero degli Dei, or Path of the Gods, which stretches 7.6 km (4.7 miles) between Praiano and Positano, offers amazing views of the Amalfi Coast and is a popular hike.

Ferries and Hydrofoils
One of the easiest, but more expensive, ways to get around the region is by the ferries that connect Naples, the Amalfi Coast and the islands. There are several ferry companies to choose from. From Naples to Ischia, for example, there are nearly 45 choices per day, with cheaper ferries and the more expensive but faster hydrofoils leaving from the main port all day. Trips generally range between 50 and 90 minutes depending on the destination. About 25 ferries shuttle between Naples and Capri and between Naples and Procida each day. Ferries also link Naples to Sorrento, where visitors can change to another boat going up the coast to Positano and Amalfi. The **Naples Bay Ferry** website is a comprehensive resource for planning.

Tickets are usually readily available until a few minutes before departure at the ticket windows at the port. Prices range between €12 and €30 for a one-way fare. Be sure to give yourself plenty of time to purchase tickets. Note that services are reduced on Sundays and holidays, and some may be cancelled in adverse weather.

Naples Bay Ferry
w naplesbayferry.com

PRACTICAL INFORMATION

A little local know-how goes a long way in Naples and the Amalfi Coast. Here you will find all the essential advice and information you will need to make the most out of your trip.

AT A GLANCE

CURRENCY
Euro (EUR)

AVERAGE DAILY SPEND

SAVE	SPEND	SPLURGE
€25	€50	€75

BOTTLED WATER	COFFEE	BEER	DINNER FOR TWO
€0.50	€1.00	€3.50	€45

ESSENTIAL PHRASES

Hello	Buon giorno
Goodbye	Arrivederci
Please	Per favore
Thank you	Grazie
Do you speak English?	Parla inglese?
I don't understand...	Non capisco

ELECTRICITY SUPPLY
Power sockets are type F and L, fitting two- and three-pronged plugs. Standard voltage is 220-230 volts.

Passports and Visas
Citizens of the UK, US, Canada, Australia and New Zealand do not need a visa for stays of up to three months but in future must apply in advance for the European Travel Information and Authorization System (ETIAS); roll-out has continually been postponed so check website for details. Visitors from other countries may also require an ETIAS, so check before travelling. EU nationals do not need a visa or ETIAS.
ETIAS
W etiasvisa.com
Polizia di Stato
W poliziadistato.it

Government Advice
Consult both your and the Italian government's advice before travelling. The **UK Foreign and Commonwealth Office**, the **US Department of State**, the **Australian Department of Foreign Affairs and Trade** and the Italian **Ministero della Salute** offer the latest information on security, health and local regulations.
Australian Department of Foreign Affairs and Trade
W smartraveller.gov.au
Ministero della Salute
W salute.gov.it
UK Foreign and Commonwealth Office
W gov.uk/foreign-travel-advice
US Department of State
W travel.state.gov

Customs Information
Find information on the laws relating to goods and currency taken in or out of Italy on the ENIT (Italy's national tourist board) website.
W enit.it

Insurance
We recommend that you take out a comprehensive insurance policy covering theft, loss of belongings, medical care, cancellation and delays.

Ensure you always read the small print carefully.

EU, UK and Australian citizens are eligible for free emergency medical care in Italy provided they have a valid European Health Insurance Card **(EHIC)** or UK Global Health Insurance Card **(GHIC)** or are registered to **Medicare**.

GHIC
Ⓦ ghic.org.uk
Medicare
Ⓦ humanservices.gov.au/individuals/medicare

Vaccinations
No inoculations are needed for Naples.

Booking Accommodation
A range of accommodation, from farm stays *(agriturismi)* to luxury hotels, can be found in the region. In the summer, accommodation fills up quickly and prices are often inflated, so book in advance. Hotels will often charge an additional city tax on top of the room price. By law, hotels are required to register guests at police headquarters and issue a receipt of payment *(ricevuta fiscale)*, which you must keep until you leave Italy.

Money
Goods and services are cheaper in Naples than on the Amalfi Coast and the islands. Most places accept major credit, debit and pre-paid currency cards, but carry cash for smaller items and street markets. ATMs *(bancomat)* are available outside most banks, which are plentiful in Naples although less so in smaller villages. Tipping is not expected for wait staff. Hotel porters and housekeeping will expect €1 per bag or day.

Travellers with Specific Requirements
Naples and the Amalfi Coast can be a challenge for travellers with specific requirements. Cobbled streets, steep staircases and a lack of elevators are all common hurdles. The islands tend to be a bit easier to navigate than

the city, though transport should be organized in advance. **Sage Traveling** and **WheelchairTraveling** are useful resources. Some sights, such as the Museo Archeologico Nazionale di Napoli, offer tactile tours and guides in braille for the visually impaired. Italian Sign Language tours are also available in Pompeii.

Sage Traveling
Ⓦ sagetraveling.com
WheelchairTraveling
Ⓦ wheelchairtraveling.com/naples-italy-wheelchair-accessible-travel-tips

Language
While Neapolitans speak Italian, the local dialect will seem unfamiliar even to native Italian speakers. Do not expect English in every establishment, especially in quieter areas on the coast and on the islands, although tourist sights are generally staffed by those who speak some English.

Opening Hours
Museums in Naples are typically open from 9am to 7:30pm, but many will close for at least one day per week, usually a Tuesday or Wednesday. Some smaller museums and galleries may also be reservation-only.

Most shops are open Monday through Saturday from 10am to 2pm and 3pm to 7pm or 8pm. Some shops in the main shopping areas in Naples may have longer hours and not close for lunch, but smaller shops outside the city will typically close for an hour in the afternoon. On Sundays, some small shops may be closed, but more shops are opening seven days a week.

Shops and museums are typically closed on public holidays.

> Situations can change quickly and unexpectedly. Always check before visiting attractions and hospitality venues for up-to-date opening hours and booking requirements.

Personal Security

Naples is a relatively safe city, but be wary of pickpockets on public transport and in crowded areas, especially around markets. Most areas of Naples feel safe during the day, but, as in any city, caution should be exercised at night. Some of the city's economically weaker neighbourhoods are still navigating the threat of local gang violence.

If you have anything stolen, report the crime to the nearest police station within 24 hours and take ID with you. If you need to make an insurance claim, get a copy of the crime report (*denuncia*). Contact your embassy if you have your passport stolen, or in the event of a serious crime or accident.

Homosexuality was legalized in Italy in 1887, and in 1982, Italy became the third country to recognize the right to legally change your gender. However, the southern regions, including Naples, are less open about LGBTQ+ relationships. While overt displays of affection may receive glances from locals, LGBTQ+ travellers should not feel unsafe, especially in the more touristy parts of the city, the Amalfi Coast and Capri. The main national LGBTQ+ organization, **ArciGay**, has a branch in Naples and provides information on events, as well as bars and clubs – Piazza Bellini is Naples' main LGBTQ+ nightlife hub.

Women may receive unwanted attention, especially around tourist areas. If you feel threatened, head for the nearest police station.

ArciGay
Ⓦ arcigaynapoli.org

Health

Italy has a world-class healthcare system. Emergency medical care in Italy is free for all EU, UK and Australian citizens. If you have an EHIC or GHIC (p127), be sure to present this as soon as possible. You may have to pay after treatment and reclaim the money later.

For visitors from outside the EU and Australia, payment of medical expenses is the patient's responsibility. It is therefore important to arrange comprehensive medical insurance before you travel. Seek medicinal supplies and advice for minor ailments from pharmacies (*farmacia*), which are found throughout the region.

AT A GLANCE

EMERGENCY NUMBERS

GENERAL EMERGENCY	POLICE
112	**113**

FIRE SERVICE	AMBULANCE
115	**118**

TIME ZONE
CET/CEST: Central European Summer Time runs from the last Sunday in March to the last Sunday in October.

TAP WATER
While tap water is generally considered safe, Neapolitans tend to drink bottled water, which is cheap and readily available.

WEBSITES AND APPS

Napoli Unplugged
Detailed website featuring insider tips (*napoliunplugged.com*).

ENIT
The official website of ENIT (*italia.com*), Italy's national tourism board.

InCampania
Naples' official tourism office (*incampania.com*) for the whole region.

Trenitalia
The Trenitalia app makes last-minute train bookings convenient.

Smoking, Alcohol and Drugs

Smoking is banned in enclosed public places, though some locals do not adhere strictly to these rules. The possession of illegal drugs is prohibited and could result in a prison sentence.

Italy has a strict limit of 0.05 per cent BAC (blood alcohol content) for drivers. This means that you cannot drink more than a small beer or a small glass of wine if you plan to drive. For drivers with less than three years' driving experience, and those under 21, the limit is 0.

ID

By law you must carry identification at all times in Italy. A photocopy of your passport photo page (and visa if applicable) should suffice. If you are stopped by the police you may be asked to present the original within 12 hours.

Local Customs

Strangers usually shake hands, while friends and family greet each other with a kiss on each cheek. Establishments called "bars" are not just for alcoholic drinks but also for coffee. At outdoor tables, waiters will usually come to newly seated patrons. It is normal to ask for the bill afterwards if the server does not bring it to the table immediately, and a simple raised hand and eye contact should do the trick.

Responsible Travel

Overtourism is having a stark impact on many of the Amalfi Coast's most scenic spots, with crowds of domestic and international tourists. If possible, try to avoid the busier months of July and August, when local infrastructure is most congested.

The roads out of Naples and around the coast get incredibly congested in summer. You can do your bit by making use of the excellent public transport network where possible, with trains connecting Naples with most of the popular sights on the coast.

Mobile Phones and Wi-Fi

Wi-Fi is generally widely available throughout the region, and cafés and restaurants will usually give you the password for their Wi-Fi if you make a purchase. Visitors travelling to Italy with EU tariffs are able to use their devices without being affected by roaming charges – they will pay the same rates for data, SMS and voice calls as they would pay at home.

Post

Stamps (*francobolli*) are sold at tobacconists (*tabacchi*) – look for a blue sign with a white T. Italian post is notorious for its unreliability. Letters and postcards can take anything between four days and two weeks to arrive, depending on the destination. The private postal services with yellow letterboxes at shops and stalls cost more and usually take longer.

Taxes and Refunds

VAT (called IVA in Italy) is usually 22 per cent, with a reduced rate of 4–10 per cent on some items. Non-EU citizens can claim an IVA rebate subject to certain conditions.

It is easier to claim before you buy; you will need to show your passport to the shop assistant and complete a form. If claiming retrospectively, at the airport, present a customs officer with your purchases and a *fattura* receipt, with your name and the amount of IVA on the item purchased.

Discount Cards

The **Naples Pass** offers discounts on entry to some main sights, city tours and well-known restaurants. The **Campania Artecard** covers an astonishingly long list of sights across the region in addition to local transport across the region. Check the website to decide which suits you best.

Campania Artecard
w campaniartecard.it
Naples Pass
w naplespass.eu/en

PLACES TO STAY

Naples feels like a city preserved in time, and never is this more apparent than when booking a place to stay. Many of the city's hotels are housed in stunning palazzi or grand repurposed villas dating from the 13th century to the belle époque. For a chic, contemporary stay, head beyond the city to the resort towns of the Amalfi Coast.

Rates are usually quoted without tourist tax, which varies by star rating and is charged per person per night. Breakfast may incur an additional cost.

PRICE CATEGORIES
For a standard, double room per night (with breakfast if included), taxes and extra charges.

€ under €130
€€ €130–€270
€€€ over €270

Naples

Costantinopoli 104

🅐 Via S. M. di Costantinopoli 104
🅦 costantinopoli104.it · €€

A rich medley of historic styles and periods – much like Naples itself – this chic hotel with stained-glass windows and wrought-iron features is housed in a Liberty-style mansion in the historic centre. The building once belonged to the aristocratic Spinelli di Fuscaldo family, and they spared no expense in adding every luxury: rooms with large balconies overlook sweeping gardens and a delightful pool.

Eurostars Hotel Excelsior

🅐 Via Partenope 48
🅦 eurostarshotels.co.uh/eurostars-hotel-excelsior.html · €€

Built in 1908 to cater for the city's most esteemed visitors, the stunning belle époque Excelsior commands views of the entire bay, Vesuvius and nearby Castel dell'Ovo.

The grande dame of Naples' plush lodgings, it featured prominently in HBO's *The Sopranos*. The hotel's classicism is evident in stylish furnishings, Murano glass lamps and Carrara marble floors. But the most important thing? It has the some of the comfiest beds you'll find in the city.

Grand Hotel Parker's

🅐 Corso Vittorio Emanuele 135 🅦 grandhotelparhers.it · €€€

This fine spot makes no bones about its illustrious pedigree. The city's first luxury hotel and formerly a Grand Tour stopover, Parker's is overflowing with priceless antiques, shimmering chandeliers and spacious rooms with sea views. Literary types are in excellent company here: the writers Robert Louis Stevenson, Virginia Woolf and Oscar Wilde all graced the hotel's hallowed halls (and its library is packed full of antiquarian books).

Hotel Caravaggio

🅐 Piazza Cardinale Sisto Riario Sforza 157
🅦 caravaggiohotel.it · €

Keen to immerse yourself in the beautiful chaos of central Naples? This humble hotel is housed in a restored 17th-century building in the lively heart of the old centre. Through the windows, you'll hear the bells tolling from the cathedral of San Gennaro, and, in the mornings, you'll catch the mouthwatering aroma of the day's first *sfogliatelle*. Caravaggio's masterwork, *Seven Works of Mercy*, is located just down the road at the Misericordia.

Grand Hotel Vesuvio

🅐 Via Partenope 45
🅦 vesuvio.it · €€

Another of the city's esteemed seafront hotels, Vesuvio was destroyed in World War II but restored to its original grandeur in the 1950s. The roster of luxury features is too long to list: two restaurants, a gym, an indoor pool, hot tub, bar and garage – there's even a chauffeur service. If you do manage to drag yourself from Veusvio's luxurious confines, you're in a great place to walk the city's seafront *lungomare*.

Grand Hotel Santa Lucia

🏠 Via Partenope 46
🌐 santalucia.it · €€

Dating back to 1906, this was the first Liberty-style hotel built in Naples. The city has long had a fondness for luxurious lodgings that sit just on the right side of gaudy, and this hotel is a perfect example. Expect antique mirrors, huge sea-facing windows and grand staircases.

Hotel Paradiso

🏠 Via Catullo 11 🌐 hotel paradisonapoli.it · €

Perched atop Posillipo Hill, far from the noise and chaos of the city, Paradiso is ideal for those who don't mind a short climb. And if the relative peace isn't reward enough for making the trek, the view of Vesuvius from the hotel's renowned Terrazzo Paradiso restaurant certainly will be. A BW Signature Collection hotel might not differ markedly from other affordable chain properties near the Mediterranean, but why mess with a winning formula?

Hotel Pignatelli

🏠 Via S. Giovanni Maggiore Pignatelli 16
🌐 hotelpignatelli napoli.com · €

One of the city's many charms is that historic stays don't always break the bank. Take this place: right in the heart of the centre, Pignatelli was once the property of the wealthy Marquis Fabrizio Pignatelli, former Governor of Naples. This illustrious history is still visible in the hotel's decoration, redolent of a time when Naples ruled its own republic. Look out for original paintings and coffered ceilings; this is a living piece of history.

Palazzo Caracciolo

🏠 Via Carbonara 112
🌐 palazzocaracciolo.com · €

Few of the city's hotels have a history stretching back quite this far. This regal building was built in the 13th century on the foundations of a pre-existing military fort and was once home to the King of Naples. Despite this, the hotel now prides itself on its decidedly modern conveniences, including a gym, spa, Jacuzzi and Turkish bath.

Amalfi Coast

Camping Zeus, Pompeii

🏠 Via Villa dei Misteri 3
🌐 campingzeus.it · €

A stay at this campsite within walking distance of the archaeological site of Pompeii is sure to fire imaginations. Perching under canvas with the looming presence of Vesuvius in the distance and a wealth of un-excavated treasures underground is a special experience. For more concrete joys, there's a bar, a restaurant and shop, as well as bunga-lows for those in need of creature comforts.

Hotel Villa Maria, Ravello

🏠 Via Trinità 14
🌐 villamaria.it · €€€

Owned and run by the Palumbo family for four generations, this villa in the heart of Ravello has its own winery stocking the finest vintages. It also offers cookery courses to induct you into the magic of a southern Italian kitchen. With so many trained chefs at hand, it goes without saying that the onsite restaurant is sublime.

Hotel Luna Convento, Amalfi

🏠 Via Pantaleone Comite 33 🌐 lunahotel.it · €€€

A spectacular example of Moorish architecture, this former convent perches vertiginously on the side of a cliff, just a short walk from Amalfi's centre. The guest rooms surround a 13th-century courtyard, with a pool, two restaurants and the splendid Moon Gardens with their shaded walks.

Holidays Baia D'Amalfi, Amalfi

🏠 Via Matteo Camera, 5
🌐 reginellahotel.it · €

Unlike in some of the smaller towns on this storied coastline, staying in comfort in Amalfi doesn't have to come at a huge cost. Holidays Baia D'Amalfi sits just a short walk from the ferry terminal in the heart of the town. Many of its rooms have excellent sea views, and the staff are happy to meet guests straight off the ferry.

Hotel Reginella, Positano

🏠 Viale Pasitea, 154
🌐 reginellahotel.it · €€

Hotels don't come cheap in chic Positano, but this family-run boutique is a more wallet-friendly alternative to the town's lavish joints. That's not to say Reginella scrimps on luxury: tucked between ramshackle hillside houses and independent shops, the hotel has a range of beautifully decorated rooms and suites. Book a superior room if you want a sea view.

Belmond Hotel Caruso, Ravello

🏠 Piazza San Giovanni del Toro 2 🌐 belmond.com/ hotels/europe/italy/ amalfi-coast/belmond- hotel-caruso · €€€

Hotel Caruso offers the definitive Ravello retreat. As you dip in the huge infinity pool or lounge with a book on the sea-facing terrace, you'll understand why the Amalfi Coast has been restoring travellers for over 2,000 years. Everything here is finely tuned to ensure perfect relaxation, from the gentle symphonic music played by the pool side to the local, nourishing dishes served in the superb restaurant.

Le Sirenuse, Positano

🏠 Via Cristoforo Colombo 30 🌐 sirenuse.it · €€€

A palatial establishment decorated with vibrant majolica tiles and kitted out with an array of antiques, Le Sirenuse is a destination in and of itself. Within its grand walls you'll find an oyster bar, a Michelin-starred restaurant, a swimming pool, a hammam and a fitness centre, not to mention a gallery's worth of fine paintings.

Monastero Santa Rosa Hotel, Conca dei Marini

🏠 Via Roma 2 🌐 monast erosantarosa.com · €€€

Originally a Dominican monastery built in the 17th century, Monastero Santa Rosa lies in the small fishing village of Conca dei Marini, conveniently located between Amalfi and Positano. A luxurious adult-only hotel perched on a cliff, it offers panoramic views of the Gulf of Salerno. Perfect for a quieter break, away from the bustle of the larger towns.

Sorrentine Peninsula

Hotel La Primavera, Massa Lubrense

🏠 Via IV Novembre 3G
🌐 laprimavera.biz
· €€

This restaurant-hotel, perched on a rocky spur and surrounded by olive groves, offers great views of the Gulf of Naples. There are no modern frills or lavish displays of luxury here, just great service in a perfect setting.

Hotel Mega Mare, Vico Equense

🏠 Corso Caulino 74
🌐 hotelmegamare.com
· €

Tucked away in the quietest spot on the Sorrento coast, Hotel Mega Mare is set high on a cliffside. Facilities include an excellent swimming pool, a well-stocked bar and a terrace solarium. A day spent relaxing by the pool or lounging at the nearby beach club? Tricky decisions like this are what coastal breaks are all about.

La Medusa, Castellammare di Stabia

🏠 Passeggiata Archeologica 5 🌐 lame dusahotel.com · €€€

This grand country villa has an array of elegant touches, from terracotta vases decorating the gate to the busts of Roman rulers, as well as gardens, fountains and a pool. A hotel fit for a Roman emperor.

Hotel Nice, Sorrento

🏠 Corso Italia 257
🌐 hotelnicesorrento.com · €€

Small and simple, this family-friendly hotel is in the town centre near the bus and train stations. It's more likely to attract those in hiking boots than high heels, with many backpackers staying, though the hotel is an upgrade from a basic hostel. It's just a short walk to Marina Grande beach, too.

Salerno Experience Hostel

🏠 Piazza Sedile del Campo 3 🌐 salerno experience.wixsite.com/ hostel · €

Located just five minutes from the beach in pretty Salerno's historic centre, this hostel has free WiFi, a roof terrace, a shared kitchen and a lounge. It offers accommodation in a private room, shared room and two dorms. The perfect place to meet other travellers.

Seven Hostel, Sorrento

🏠 Via Iommella Grande, Sant'Agnello 🌐 seven hostel.eu · €

For those more into hiking than haute cuisine, this hostel offers a perfectly simple base from which to walk the undulating coastline. Housed in an 18th-

century building, it has private rooms and 12 dorms along with all amenities, including a restaurant, café-bar and a large roof terrace.

Capri

Jumeirah Capri Palace

🏠 Via Capodimonte 14
🌐 jumeirah.com/en/stay/ italy/capri-palace-jumeirah · €€€

Think it overly boastful to call a hotel a palace? You haven't stayed at Jumeirah. With service of the very highest quality, the whole place is designed to dazzle. The beauty and spa treatments are excellent, some suites have their own pools, and the hotel's L'Olivo has two Michelin stars.

La Prora

🏠 Via Castello 6/8
🌐 albergolaprora.it · €€€

A small hotel in the centre of the medieval district, La Prora is just a five-minute walk from the Piazzetta. All the rooms have been modelled in a classic minimalist style. Book ahead if you want a room with a balcony.

Island Charmers

Casa Bormioli - Maison de Charme, Procida

🏠 Via Principe Umberto 86
🌐 casabormioli.it · €

This elegant B&B offers air-conditioned rooms just a stone's throw from

La Chiaia beach. Notice something unique as you enter? Each room is lovingly decorated with objects brought back by the owners from their travels, just one homely touch that sets this fine spot apart.

La Casa sul Mare, Procida

🏠 Via Salita Castello 13, Corricella 🌐 lacasa sulmare.it · €

Housed in a renovated building dating from 1700, this hotel sits at the foot of the acropolis of Terra Murata, making it a perfect place to connect with Procida's ancient roots.

Hotel Ulisse, Ischia

🏠 Via Champault 9, Ischia Porto 🌐 hotelulisse.com · €

Located in the Borgo dei Pescatori, close to the beach and the town centre, Hotel Ulisse offers a wonderful view of the Aragonese Castle, which is best admired from the lush waters of the hotel pool.

Il Moresco, Ischia

🏠 Via E Gianturco 16, Ischia Porto 🌐 ilmoresco.it/en · €€€

Situated in the most beautiful corner of the island, this five-star hotel is the meeting point for well-heeled clientele. The refined villa is set in a park surrounding a thermal pool, and is just a few steps away from its own private beach.

INDEX

PHRASE BOOK

In an Emergency

Help!	Aiuto!	eye-yoo-toh
Stop!	Ferma!	fair-mah
Call a doctor	Chiama un medico	kee-ah-mah oon meh-deekoh
Call an ambulance	Chiama un' ambulanza	kee-ah-mah oon am-boo-lan-tsa
Call the police	Chiama la polizia	kee-ah-mah lah pol-ee-tsee-ah
Call the fire brigade	Chiama i pompieri	kee-ah-mah ee pom-pee-air-ee

Communication Essentials

Yes/No	Sì/No	see/noh
Please	Per favore	pair fah-vor-eh
Thank you	Grazie	grah-tsee-eh
Excuse me	Mi scusi	mee skoo-zee
Good morning	Buongiorno	bwon jor-noh
Goodbye	Arrivederci	ah-ree-veh-dair-chee
Good evening	Buona sera	bwon-ah sair-ah
What?	Che?	keh
When?	Quando?	kwan-doh
Why?	Perché?	pair-keh
Where?	Dove?	doh-veh

Useful Phrases

How are you?	Come sta?	koh-meh stah
Very well, thank you.	Molto bene, grazie.	moll-toh beh-neh grah-tsee-eh
Pleased to meet you.	Piacere di conoscerla.	pee-ah-chair-eh dee coh-noh-shair-lah
That's fine.	Va bene.	va beh-neh
Where is/are...?	Dov'è/ Dove sono...?	dov-eh/ doveh soh-noh
How do I get to...?	Come faccio per arrivare a...?	koh-meh fah-cho pair arri-var-eh a
Do you speak English?	Parla inglese?	par-lah een-gleh-zeh
I don't understand.	Non capisco.	non ka-pee-skoh
I'm sorry.	Mi dispiace.	mee dee-spee-ah-cheh

Shopping

How much does this cost?	Quanto, costa?	kwan-toh kostah
I would like...	Vorrei...	vor-ray
Do you have...?	Avete...?	ah-veh-teh
Do you take credit cards?	Accettate carte di credito?	ah-chet-tah-teh kar-teh dee creh-dee-toh
What time do you open/close?	A che ora apre/ chiude?	a keh ora ah-preh/ kee-oo-deh
this one	questo	kweh-stoh
that one	quello	kwell-oh
expensive	caro	kar-oh
cheap	economico	ee-con-om-ee-coh
size (clothes)	la taglia	lah tah-lee-ah
size (shoes)	il numero	eel noo-mair-oh
white	bianco	bee-ang-koh
black	nero	neh-roh
red	rosso	ross-oh
yellow	giallo	jal-loh
green	verde	vair-deh
blue	blu	bloo

Types of Shop

bakery	il forno/ panificio	eel forn-oh/ panee-fee-cho
bank	la banca	lah bang-kah
bookshop	la libreria	lah lee-breh-ree-ah
cake shop	la pasticceria	lah pas-tee-chair-ee-ah
chemist	la farmacia	lah far-mah-chee-ah
delicatessen	la salumeria	lah sah-loo-meh-ree-ah
department store	il grande magazzino	eel gran-deh ma-gad-zeenoh
grocery	il negozio di alimentari	eel ne-gots-yo dee ah-lee-mentah-ree
hairdresser	il parrucchiere	eel par-oo-kee-air-eh
ice-cream parlour	la gelateria	lah jel-lah-tair-ree-ah
market	il mercato	eel mair-kah-toh
newsstand	l'edicola	leh-dee-koh-lah
post office	l'ufficio postale	loo-fee-choh pos-tah-leh
supermarket	il supermercato	eel su-pair-mair-kah-toh
tobacconist	il tabaccaio	eel tah-bak-eye-oh
travel agency	l'agenzia di viaggi	lah-jen-tsee-ah dee vee-ad-jee

Sightseeing

art gallery	la pinacoteca	lah peena-koh-teh-kah
bus stop	la fermata dell'autobus	lah fair-mah-tah dell-ow-toh-booss
church	la chiesa/ basilica	lah kee-en-zah bah-seel-ee-kah
closed for holidays	chiuso per ferie	kee-oo-zoh pair fair-ee-eh
garden	il giardino	eel jar-dee-no
museum	il museo	eel moo-zeh-oh
railway station	la stazione	lah stah-tsee-oh-neh
tourist information	l'ufficio del turismo	loo-fee-choh del too-ree-smoh

Staying in a Hotel

Do you have any vacant rooms?	Avete camere libere?	ah-veh-teh kah-mair-eh lee-bair-eh
double room	una camera doppia	oona kah-mairah doh-pee-ah
with double bed	con letto matrimoniale	kon let-toh mah-tree-moh-nee-ah-leh
a room with bath/ shower	una camera con bagno/ doccia	oona ka-mair-ah kon ban-yo/ dot-chah
twin room	una camera con due letti	oona kah-mairah kon doo-eh let-tee
single room	una camera singola	oona kah-mairah sing-goh-lah
I have a reservation	Ho una prenotazione	oh oona preh-noh-tah-tsee-oh-neh

Eating Out

Have you got a table for…?	Avete un tavolo per…?	ah-veh-teh oon tah-voh-loh pair
I'd like to reserve a table	Vorrei prenotare un tavolo	vor-ray pre-noh-ta-reh oon tah-voh-loh
breakfast	colazione	koh-lah-tsee-oh-neh
lunch	pranzo	pran-tsoh
dinner	cena	cheh-nah
the bill	il conto	eel kon-toh
waitress	cameriera	kah-mair-ee-air-ah
waiter	cameriere	kah-mair-ee-air-eh
fixed-price menu	il menù a prezzo fisso	eel meh-noo ah pret-soh fee-soh
dish of the day	piatto del giorno	pee-ah-toh dell jor-no
starter	l'antipasto	lan-tee-pass-toh
first course	il primo	eel pree-moh
main course	il secondo	eel seh-kon-doh
sides	i contorni	ee kon-tor-noh
dessert	il dolce	eel doll-cheh
wine list	la lista dei vini	lah lee-stah day vee-nee
glass	il bicchiere	eel bee-kee-air-eh
bottle	la bottiglia	lah bot-teel-yah
knife	il coltello	eel kol-tell-oh
fork	la forchetta	lah for-ket-tah
spoon	il cucchiaio	eel koo-kee-eye-oh

Menu Decoder

l'acqua minerale	lah-kwah meenair-ah-leh	mineral water
gassata/ naturale	gah-zah-tah/ nah-too-rah-leh	fizzy still
l'agnello	lah-niell-oh	lamb
l'aglio	lal-ee-oh	garlic
al forno	al for-noh	baked
alla griglia	ah-lah greel-yah	grilled
la birra	lah beer-rah	beer
la bistecca	lah bee-stek-ah	steak
il burro	eel boor-oh	butter
il caffè	eel kah-feh	coffee
la carne	la kar-neh	meat
carne di maiale	kar-neh dee mah-yah-leh	pork
la cipolla	la chip-oh-lah	onion
il formaggio	eel for-mad-joh	cheese
le fragole	leh frah-goh-leh	strawberries
il fritto misto	eel free-toh mees-toh	mixed fried food
la frutta	la froot-tah	fruit
frutti di mare	froo-tee dee mah-reh	seafood
i funghi	ee foon-ghee	mushrooms
i gamberi	ee gam-bair-ee	prawns
il gelato	eel jel-lah-toh	ice cream
l'insalata	leen-sah-lah-tah	salad
il latte	eel laht-teh	milk
il manzo	eel man-tsoh	beef
l'olio	loh-lee-oh	oil
il pane	eel pah-neh	bread
le patate	leh pah-tah-teh	potatoes
le patatine fritte	leh pah-tah-teen-eh free-teh	chips
il pepe	eel peh-peh	pepper
il pesce	eel pesh-eh	fish
il pollo	eel poll-oh	chicken
il pomodoro	eel poh-moh-dor-oh	tomato
il prosciutto cotto/ crudo	eel pro-shoo-toh kot-toh/ kroo-doh	ham cooked/ cured
il riso	eel ree-zoh	rice
il sale	eel sah-leh	salt
la salsiccia	lah sal-see-chah	sausage
il succo d'arancia	eel soo-koh dah-ran-chah	orange juice
il tè	eel teh	tea
la torta	lah tor-tah	cake/tart
l'uovo	loo-oh-voh	egg
vino bianco	vee-noh bee-ang-koh	white wine
vino rosso	vee-noh ross-oh	red wine
lo zucchero	loh zoo-kair-oh	sugar
la zuppa	lah tsoo-pah	soup

Time

one minute	un minuto	oon mee-noo-toh
one hour	un'ora	oon or-ah
a day	un giorno	oon jor-noh
Monday	lunedì	loo-neh-dee
Tuesday	martedì	mar-teh-dee
Wednesday	mercoledì	mair-koh-leh-dee
Thursday	giovedì	joh-veh-dee
Friday	venerdì	ven-air-dee
Saturday	sabato	sah-bah-toh
Sunday	domenica	doh-meh-nee-ka

Numbers

1	uno	oo-noh
2	due	doo-eh
3	tre	treh
4	quattro	kwat-roh
5	cinque	ching-kweh
6	sei	say-ee
7	sette	set-teh
8	otto	ot-toh
9	nove	noh-veh
10	dieci	dee-eh-chee
11	undici	oon-dee-chee
17	diciassette	dee-chah-set-teh
18	diciotto	dee-chot-toh
19	diciannove	dee-cha-noh-veh
20	venti	ven-tee
30	trenta	tren-tah
40	quaranta	kwah-ran-tah
50	cinquanta	ching-kwan-tah
60	sessanta	sess-an-tah
70	settanta	set-tan-tah
80	ottanta	ot-tan-tah
90	novanta	noh-van-tah
100	cento	chen-toh
1,000	mille	mee-leh

ACKNOWLEDGMENTS

This edition updated by

Contributors Toni de Bella, Carol King

Senior Editor Alison McGill

Senior Designers Stuti Tiwari, Laura O'Brien

Project Editors Alex Pathe, Anuroop Sanwwalia

Editor Ishita Chaterjee

Proofreader Elly Dowsett

Indexer Gina Guilinger

Picture Research Deputy Manager
Virien Chopra

Assistant Picture Research Administrator
Manpreet Kaur

Rights and Permissions Specialist Priya Singh

Publishing Assistant Simona Velikova

Jacket Designers Laura O'Brien

Senior Cartographic Editors
Subhashree Bharati, James Macdonald

Cartography Manager Suresh Kumar

Senior DTP Designer Tanveer Zaidi

DTP Designer Rohit Rojal

Senior Production Controller Samantha Cross

Managing Editor Beverley Smart

Managing Art Editor Gemma Doyle

Senior Managing Art Editor Priyanka Thakur

Art Director Maxine Pedliham

Editorial Director Hollie Teague

Publishing Director Georgina Dee

DK would like to thank the following for their contribution to the previous editions: Jeffrey Kennedy, Laura Thayer, Alessandra Pugliesi.

The publisher would like to thank the following for their kind permission to reproduce their photographs:

Key: a-above; b-below/bottom; c-center; f-far; l-left; r-right; t-top

4Corners: Massimo Ripani 19

Adobe Stock: Marco 20ca, Maurizio De Mattei 21cr, 116t, SeanPavonePhoto 74b, Takashi Images 116b, Wirestock Creators 53b

Alamy Stock Photo: AGF Srl / Antonio Capone 77, Art Collection 2 57t, Art Kowalsky 70, ARTGEN 37, Associated Press 11t, Azoor Photo Collection 29ca, Bailey-Cooper Photography 27, Bildagentur-online / Joko 89, Kevin Britland 68, Richard Broadwell 111, Browny 17, CBW 8cl, Classic Image 9br, Roy Conchie 16clb, Ian Dagnall 52, Lorenzo Dalberto 28, Bennett Dean 24b, Adam Eastland 21t, 35tr, 66, Peter Eastland 29tl, Richard Ellis 53t, Cormon Francis / Hemis.fr 78, Stu G 62b, GL Archive 30t, Jeremy Graham 99, Hackenberg-Photo-Cologne 96, Gardel Bertrand / Hemis.fr 71, Hauser Patrice / Hemis.fr 23br, 33tr, 98, Hughes Hervé / Hemis.fr 88, Maisant Ludovic / Hemis.fr 94, Peter Horree 9tr, 29ca, 79, Image Professionals GmbH / LOOK-foto 72t, 112, Imagebroker / Arco / B. Bönsch 41, imageBROKER / Guenter Graefenhain 12crb, 45, imageBROKER.com GmbH & Co. KG / Fabian von Poser 16tr, incamerastock 56, Independent Photo Agency Srl 87, INTERFOTO / History 10tl, 10tr, INTERFOTO / Travel 13tl, Jon Arnold Images Ltd / Michele Falzone 44, Julia Catt Photography 36, Marka / Massimiliano Bonatti 91, Barry Mason 10clb, mauritius images GmbH / verano 9cr, mauritius images GmbH / ClickAlps 61, Sérgio Nogueira 23crb, M. Timothy O'Keefe 13clb, Berk Ozdemir 51, Panther Media GmbH / verano 9cr, Paolo Reda - REDA &CO / Alfio Giannotti 47cl, 86, peter.forsberg 15cr, Prisma Archivo 32cl, Stefano Ravera 22, 23cb, Realy Easy Star / Giuseppe Masci 25b, David Ridley 15cl, eobertharding / Frank Fell 12br, James Schwabel 85, Science History Images 8b, Peter Forsberg / Shopping 73b, Lourens Smak 113, James Talalay 54t, The Color Archives 10cl, The Picture Art Collection 9tl, Theodore Thomas 59t, Ivan Vdovin 101, Westend61 GmbH / Martin Moxter 102

AWL Images: Marco Bottigelli 5, Neil Farrin 42, Stefano Politi Markovina 49, 106

Bowinkel: Uberto Bowinkel 97

Carthusia: 110

Depositphotos Inc: mikolajn 43bl, wirestock_creators 118

Dreamstime.com: 22tomtom 65b, Alexirina27000 93t, Beataaldridge 67, Ivan Vander Biesen 57b, Marco Brivio 26b, Tatiana Chekryzhova 72b, Daliu80 16ca, Dorinmarius 62-63t, Engin Korkmaz 24-25t, Vladimir Korostyshevskiy 30b, 35b, 93b, Giambattista Lazazzera 117, Lucamato 69b, Mariyasiyanko 119, Massimobuonaiuto 76, Mitzobs 26cl, Danilo Mongiello 47br, Anna Pakutina 83b, Pfeifferv 108, Photogolfer 83t, 95, Roman Plesky 109, Dzianis Rabtsevich 38-39t, Michele Renzullo 38b, Valerio Rosati 75, Adriano Spano 13bl, Andrei Stancu 43cb, Alvaro German Vilela 121, Wirestock 69t, Xantana 105

Getty Images: Corbis Documentary / Maremagnum 16cla, De Agostini 29tr, De

A NOTE FROM DK

The rate at which the world is changing is constantly keeping the DK travel team on our toes. While we've worked hard to ensure that this edition of Naples and the Amalfi Coast is accurate and up-to-date, we know that opening hours alter, standards shift, prices fluctuate, places close and new ones pop up in their stead. So, if you notice we've got something wrong or left something out, we want to hear about it. Please get in touch at travelguides@dk.com

Within each Top 10 list in this book, no hierarchy of quality or popularity is implied. All 10 are, in the editor's opinion, of roughly equal merit.

First edition 2004

Published in Great Britain by Dorling
Kindersley Limited, DK, 20 Vauxhall Bridge Road,
London SW1V 2SA

The authorised representative in the EEA is
Dorling Kindersley Verlag GmbH. Arnulfstr.
124, 80636 Munich, Germany

Published in the United States by DK Publishing,
1745 Broadway, 20th Floor, New York, NY 10019, USA

Copyright © 2004, 2025 Dorling Kindersley Limited
A Penguin Random House Company

25 26 27 28 10 9 8 7 6 5 4 3 2 1

A CIP catalog record for this book
is available from the British Library.

A catalog record for this book is available
from the Library of Congress.

ISSN: 1542 1554
ISBN: 978 0 2417 1975 6

Printed and bound in China

www.dk.com